TOLKIEN

HOW AN OBSCURE OXFORD PROFESSOR
WROTE *THE HOBBIT* AND BECAME
THE MOST BELOVED AUTHOR
OF THE CENTURY

DEVIN BROWN

Abingdon Press
Nashville

TOLKIEN
How an Obscure Oxford Professor Wrote *The Hobbit*
and Became the Most Beloved Author of the Century

Library of Congress Cataloging-in-Publication Data

Brown, Devin.
    Tolkien : how an obscure Oxford professor wrote The Hobbit and became the most beloved author of the century / Devin Brown.
        pages cm
    ISBN 978-1-4267-9670-8 (soft back, trade pbk. : alk. paper) 1. Tolkien, J. R. R. (John Ronald Reuel), 1892-1973--Criticism and interpretation. 2. Tolkien, J. R. R. (John Ronald Reuel), 1892-1973—Appreciation 3. Tolkien, J. R. R. (John Ronald Reuel), 1892-1973. Hobbit.   4. Children's stories, English—History and criticism.   5. Fantasy fiction, English—History and criticism.   I. Title.
    PR6039.O32Z587 2014
    823'.912—dc23

                                                                                          2014033816

14 15 16 17 18 19 20 21 22 23—10 9 8 7 6 5 4 3 2 1
MANUFACTURED IN THE UNITED STATES OF AMERICA

CONTENTS

PROLOGUE

As the final weeks of the twentieth century drew to a close and the first day of 2000 approached, the attention of the entire world, or so it seemed, was focused on three questions.

The first had to do with a problem known as Y2K. Would all the technology created in the previous one hundred years suddenly crash at the stroke of midnight? Back then memory bits were more expensive, and to save space early software had been designed to record the year with only two digits. The fear was that all over the world, computers, power grids, municipal water supplies, and even microwave ovens would simply stop working as their internal calendars marking the year rolled from 99 back to 00.

Various strategies were put forward about how to prepare for the looming crisis—from stockpiling water and nonperishable food items to withdrawing large amounts of cash and staying off airplanes. But to everyone's relief, disruption from the Millennium bug, as it was also called, was largely negligible.

The second question was, for most people, far less pressing. Did the new century and new millennium really begin on January 1, 2000, or—because there had been no year 0000—shouldn't the world wait until 2001 to celebrate? Ignoring historians, mathematicians, and general spoilsports, the people of the world decided that twenty-first century and the third millennium began when *they* said it did and went out *en masse* to welcome their arrival.

The third question was a more general one. Who or what had been the best—the best of the century or even, in some cases, of the millennium? A seemingly endless flurry of polls, surveys, Top 10, Top 50, and Top 100 lists were compiled. And when it came to the best book or best author of the past hundred years, in poll after poll, survey after survey, list after list—J. R. R. Tolkien was always at the top.

At Waterstones, the giant British bookstore, *The Lord of the Rings* was declared the book of the century after it received the most votes at 104 of the store's 105 branches—the lone exception being the branch where James Joyce's *Ulysses* came in first and *The Lord of the Rings* second. Also ranking high among vote-getters in Waterstones's Top Books of the Century, *The Hobbit* came in at number nineteen.

When *The Daily Telegraph* asked readers across the United Kingdom to vote for their favorite author and favorite book, Tolkien and *The Lord of the Rings* won again. The members of the Folio Society, also in England, ranked *The Lord of the Rings* first, with *Pride and Prejudice* second. Tolkien's epic was at the top of a poll taken by the BBC to determine the "Nation's Best-Loved Book" and was at the top of similar polls in Australia and Germany.

Not to be outdone, in a poll conducted in the U.S., Amazon.com customers voted *The Lord of the Rings* as the best book of the millennium, ahead of such works as *Gone with the Wind,* which came in second; *To Kill a Mockingbird,* which came in third; and even *Harry Potter and the Sorcerer's Stone,* which took fifth. Only two authors had more than one book in Amazon's top twenty. Tolkien was one of them, with *The Hobbit* coming in at number twelve. With his *Complete Works* and *Hamlet* a little further down the list at sixteen and seventeen, William Shakespeare was the other.

In *Christianity Today*'s survey of the Best 100 Religious Books of the Century, J. R. R. Tolkien and *The Lord of the Rings* came in ahead of works by such notable Christian authors as Richard Foster, Oswald Chambers, and Reinhold Niebuhr. *The Lord of the Rings* placed first, and *The Hobbit* was number twenty-five in the BBC's Big Read list of the Top 100 Books. The teachers of the National Education Association placed *The Hobbit* in their list of 100 Best Books for Young People.

Spurred on by the three blockbuster *Hobbit* films here in

the second decade of the twenty-first century, sales of Tolkien's books continue to rise, making any assessment outdated as soon as it is given. Current estimates put sales of *The Lord of the Rings* at well over 150 million copies and sales of *The Hobbit* at well over 100 million, placing them among the best-selling books of all time. The film adaptations of Tolkien's works are among the top-grossing movies ever made and have further helped to make their characters—Bilbo Baggins, his nephew Frodo, the ever-faithful Sam Gamgee, and Gandalf the Grey—into household names.

But it was not always this way.

In fact, *The Hobbit* and *The Lord of the Rings* may without exaggeration both be described as books that very nearly weren't.

———⚬———

"You are a very fine person, Mr. Baggins, and I am very fond of you," said Gandalf. "But you are only quite a little fellow in a wide world after all!"

"Thank goodness!" said Bilbo laughing, and handed him the tobacco-jar.

The time was October 30, 1936. The place was the stately north-London suburb of Hampstead, in the comfortable family home of Stanley and Mary Unwin and their three children.

The youngest of the three, ten-year-old Rayner, read this final exchange between Gandalf and Bilbo, and thought about what he would say in his review of the strange new story he had just finished. His father, founder of the firm of Allen & Unwin, had read the story and liked it but wanted his son's input before making a final decision about whether to publish it or not.

What to say?

Though he didn't realize it at the time, ten-year-old Rayner Unwin held not just the future of this particular story in his hands, but the entire writing career of a then-unknown Oxford professor. Though no one—not the author, not the handful of friends who had seen the manuscript, and certainly not Rayner or Stanley Unwin—imagined it at the time, this book and the sequel that followed it would one day be known and loved all over the world.

What to say?

Rayner knew his opinion was taken seriously by his father. In fact, his good opinion was critical when the firm was considering publishing a book for young people. As he explained much later in an interview: "In those happy days, no second opinion was needed; if I said it was good enough to publish, it was published."

And so for a moment, the fate of *The Hobbit*—and that of *The Lord of the Rings* as well, for without *The Hobbit* there would have been no request for a sequel—was in the hands of a ten-year-old boy. What is more amazing is the fact that this was not the first time, nor would it be the last, that the literary fate of Middle-earth would depend on just one rather ordinary person.

After thinking for a minute, young Rayner made his decision. He set aside the manuscript pages and got out his paper and pen, and in his own wobbly hand began to write.

Report on "The Hobbit"

Bilbo Baggins was a Hobbit who lived in his
hobbit-hole and <u>never</u> went for adventures,
at last Gandalf the wizard and his Dwarves
persuaded him to go. He had a very exciting
time fighting goblins and wargs. At last they get
to the lonely mountain; Smaug, the dragon who
guards it is killed and after a terrific battle with
the goblins he returned home—rich!

This book, with the help of maps, does not need
any illustrations it is good and should appeal to
all children between the ages of 5 and 9.

For his report, Rayner received his usual payment of one shilling, a coin used before England's decimalization of its currency, with a value of twelve pence.

———✦———

PROLOGUE

What follows is the incredible, true story of how an obscure Oxford professor came to write first *The Hobbit* and later *The Lord of the Rings* and went on to become the most-beloved author of the century. It is a tale as amazing and inspiring as any of the fictional ones that Tolkien himself would create.

PART ONE
SON AND SCHOOLBOY

A Hot, Parched Country

Visitors to the U.K. will find tastefully understated, round plaques in a dignified shade of blue marking the birthplace of many of the country's most famous writers—figures such as Charles Dickens, Dorothy Sayers, C. S. Lewis, and Graham Greene. Although there is a plaque in the Oxford suburbs on the house at 20 Northmoor Road where J. R. R. Tolkien lived from 1930 to 1947, marking it as the very place where *The Hobbit* and *The Lord of the Rings* were written, there is no plaque marking his birthplace. His birthplace has no plaque because Tolkien was not born in Oxford or England but literally a world away in Bloemfontein in the Orange Free State, the former colony we now know as South Africa.

On January 3, 1892, just three days into the new year, John Ronald Reuel Tolkien came into the world. Born with his father's eyes and his mother's mouth, he was the first child of Arthur and Mabel Tolkien, who had recently emigrated from England. Named "John" after his grandfather, and "Reuel" because it was a family name, he would be called Ronald by his family and John Ronald by school chums. Later at Oxford, he would be Tolkien to his colleagues, and to his friends he would simply be Tollers.

Back in 1892, Bloemfontein was not quite fifty years old and not the bustling modern city it is today. Although it had two churches, a hospital, a library, a tennis club, and a railway station, it was still a dusty frontier town set on the edge of a treeless plain where wild dogs, monkeys, jackals, and the occasional lion still roamed. Tolkien later wrote that his earliest childhood memories were of a "hot parched country" and that the first Christmas he recalled was not a frosty, snow-covered morning, but a day with a blazing sun, curtains drawn against the heat, and in place of a cheerful English pine, a eucalyptus tree that was so dry it drooped.

After working for a time at Lloyds Bank in Birmingham, Arthur Tolkien had gone to South Africa, like many emigrants from England at the time, in search of a better position. Because of recent discoveries of gold and diamonds in the region, promotions in the banking business were speedier and more available there than in Britain. After a number of temporary postings, Arthur had been named as the manager of the Bloemfontein branch of the Bank of Africa. With a modest but adequate income and housing provided for him on the second floor above the bank, he felt ready to ask his young fiancée to join him.

Arthur Tolkien and Mabel Suffield were married in Cape

Town's Anglican Cathedral on April 16, 1891. She was twenty-one. He was thirty-four. After a brief honeymoon on the coast in nearby Sea Point, Arthur and "Mab," as he called his new bride, boarded a train for the arduous 700-mile trek inland to Bloemfontein to begin their new life together. Nine months later, Arthur wrote to his mother back in England with the exciting news: "Mabel gave me a beautiful little son last night."

Among the many incidents that took place during Ronald Tolkien's first years, three bear noting. First there came a day when the infant was nowhere to be found, sending the household into a panic. Some time later it was discovered that Isaak, the local boy Arthur and Mabel had hired to help around the house, without saying a word to anyone, had taken tiny John Ronald back home with him to show with wonder and pride to his family and neighbors who had never seen a white baby. After the tumult subsided, Isaak was admonished but not dismissed, and in fact, remained on such good relations with the Tolkiens that later he named his first son Isaak Mister Tolkien Victor.

Several months after his adventure with Isaak, young Ronald was stung by a tarantula as he was outside learning to walk. Following his screams, his nurse ran after him, scooped him up, and quickly sucked out the poison, saving his life. Recalling this incident later for an interview, Tolkien pointed out that despite the fact that large, evil spiders appear in both *The*

Hobbit and *The Lord of the Rings*, he did not particularly dislike spiders and even made a point of rescuing the ones that got trapped in the family bathtub.

The third memorable incident from this time was that on February 17, 1894, six weeks after his second birthday, Ronald got a new baby brother to play with when Hilary Arthur Reuel Tolkien was born.

As a small child, Ronald had trouble adjusting to the hot climate of Bloemfontein. In part because of this and in part because Mabel missed her family, it was decided that she would take the two boys back to England to visit their relatives by herself, with the understanding that Arthur would join them shortly afterwards on the scheduled furlough that had been postponed more than once already. In April 1895, four years after her arrival in Bloemfontein, Mabel made the long train ride back to Cape Town with her one-year-old and three-year-old in tow. Together with the nurse Arthur had hired to travel with them, they boarded the *S. S. Guelph* for the voyage up the Indian Ocean, through the Suez Canal, and across the Mediterranean. Three weeks later they arrived in England, the place Mabel still considered home.

Later in life Tolkien would remember looking down from the deck of a ship into the clear waters of the Indian Ocean, which were filled with agile black and brown bodies diving for coins thrown by the passengers. He would also remember the sight of a great city set high on a hill, which he later understood had been Lisbon. He also retained an image of his father, a narrow brush in hand, painting *A. R. Tolkien* on the trunk they used on the trip. It would be the last memory Ronald would have of his father. After delaying his furlough once more, Arthur contracted rheumatic fever and died of a severe hemorrhage on February 15, 1896. Five days later, his body was laid to rest in Bloemfontein's Anglican graveyard. Ronald was four, and Hilary had just turned two. Mabel was twenty-six.

Given their shortage of money and the length of travel time, Mabel and the boys were not able to be present at Arthur's funeral, nor did Tolkien ever return to the land he was born in. During World War II, his youngest son, Christopher, served in the Royal Air Force and trained in South Africa. In a letter dated April 24, 1944, Tolkien wrote him: "If you fetch up at Bloemfontein I shall wonder if the little old stone bankhouse where I was born is still standing." There is no record of whether Christopher made it to his father's birthplace. If he did, he would have discovered that the original bank building was gone, having been wiped out by a flood and replaced by a new structure built in 1933. In the early 1990s members of the South African Tolkien Society located Arthur's grave and along with the Tolkien family had a new gravestone placed on it.

With very little memory of his father, Tolkien was more

influenced by his absence than anything he had said or done. When it came time to write his fiction, fatherless characters and foster fathers would appear in key roles, notable among them Frodo, who is raised by Bilbo, and Aragorn, who is only two when his father dies and is subsequently raised by Elrond.

A Childhood Paradise

After they arrived back in England, Mabel and the boys initially stayed with her parents in the family home in the King's Heath subdivision located on Birmingham's south side. Everyone assumed the cramped living conditions would be temporary, that soon Arthur would join them, and that shortly afterwards they would again return to South Africa. Mabel's sister and brother were still at home at the time, and the addition of two small boys made life chaotic in the small house. Despite the ruckus Ronald and Hilary caused, the Suffields were glad to get the chance to spend time with their grandsons, whom they had never seen, and to have their daughter safe at home again.

After Arthur's death, Mabel knew she needed to find a more permanent living arrangement, though exactly where to go was a problem. The investments Arthur had made provided barely enough for the three of them to survive on. Coupled with the modest assistance she received from her relatives, the money would need to be stretched as far as possible. Deciding that the soot and factory smoke of Birmingham were not good for young children and that an inexpensive place in the country would at least provide the boys with a wholesome place to play, Mabel began to look for housing beyond the city's southern edge. It was not long before she found a semi-detached brick cottage for rent about a mile out in the country. As biographer Humphrey Carpenter notes, it would be a home that could make them happy in spite of their poverty.

It would also be a home that would have a great influence on Tolkien's fiction.

In the summer of 1896, Mabel and her two sons moved to Sarehole, a small hamlet consisting of a handful of farms and houses nestled alongside the equally modest River Cole. The name *Sarehole* originally came from the *holme*—the low, rich land alongside a river—belonging to *Sare*, and the area offered everything two young boys could want: fields and meadows to run in, magnificent old trees to climb, strawberries to pick, mushrooms to steal, and a mysterious mill and mill pond to explore.

The Stratford Road outside their door, which led to Birmingham in the north and to Stratford-upon-Avon in the south, was then only a narrow lane lined by farms and fields. In those days before the advance of the automobile, it would have had no traffic louder than a tradesman's wagon or a farmer's cart passing by. Later Tolkien would recall the pastoral setting of his youth and would have *The Hobbit* begin on a morning "long ago in the quiet of the world, when there was less noise and more green."

While today, due to the influence of Peter Jackson's films, Tolkien fans in search of a real-life Middle-earth often travel to New Zealand, Tolkien himself made it clear that The Shire was based on his memories of Sarehole and his experiences as a young boy living there. "I took the idea of the hobbits from the village people and children," he pointed out in an interview. "I was brought up in considerable poverty, but I was happy running about in that country."

Besides the idea of the hobbits, there were other elements from Tolkien's youth that would make it into his fiction. One was the name *Gamgee*, which would be used as Sam's last name and that of his father, Gaffer Gamgee. In 1880, Dr. Joseph Sampson Gamgee, a surgeon at Queen's Hospital in Birmingham, had invented the first medical dressing made of cotton, which became known thereafter as a Gamgee Tissue. Tolkien later explained that the name was "caught out of childhood memory" and noted that it was the association of *Gamgee* with cotton that led to his whimsical creation of the Cottons as a family Sam would be associated with and eventually marry into.

Even late in life, Tolkien was still able to remember the area around Sarehole in precise detail. "There was an old mill that really did grind corn with two millers, a great big pond with swans on it, a sandpit, a wonderful dell with flowers, a few old-fashioned village houses, and further away, a stream with another mill," he told the *Oxford Mail*. "I could draw you a map of every inch of it," he added. "It was a kind of lost paradise."

Tolkien would have this map of his childhood paradise in mind for the path Bilbo takes from Bag End as he sets off on his great adventure as readers of *The Hobbit* are told: "To the end of his days Bilbo could never remember how he found himself outside . . . pushing his keys into Gandalf's hands, and running as fast as his furry feet could carry him down the lane, past the great Mill, across The Water, and then on for a mile or more."

Visitors to Sarehole today can still find the old mill alongside the pond. A plaque marking it as Sarehole Mill records that it has been the site of a water mill since 1542 and that it served as a source of inspiration for the fiction of J. R. R. Tolkien, who lived nearby from 1896 to 1900.

Mabel had a deep fondness for plants and knew a good deal of botany, and she passed on this love and knowledge to her two boys. Her older son would later lovingly write about trees in his fiction, and Hilary would become an orchard keeper. Two of the trees that appear in Tolkien's fiction—the

Party Tree where Bilbo makes his farewell speech, only to have it felled later by Saruman's workers, and Old Man Willow—can be linked to a specific tree from his childhood in Sarehole. Tolkien recalled: "There was a willow hanging over the mill-pool and I learned to climb it. It belonged to a butcher on the Stratford Road, I think. One day they cut it down. They didn't do anything with it: the log just lay there. I never forgot that."

Tolkien's memories of Sarehole and his anguish at the urbanization that slowly spread from Birmingham to the rural countryside he so loved can be found in *The Fellowship of the Ring* in the vision of the Shire that Sam sees in the Mirror of Galadriel. Tolkien would later write:

> Like a dream the vision shifted ... and he saw
> the trees again. ... They were falling, crashing to
> the ground.
>
> "Hi!" cried Sam in an outraged voice. "There's
> that Ted Sandyman a-cutting down trees as he
> shouldn't. They didn't ought to be felled: it's
> that avenue beyond the Mill that shades the
> road to Bywater. I wish I could get at Ted, and
> I'd fell *him!*"
>
> But now Sam noticed that the Old Mill had
> vanished, and a large red-brick building was
> being put up where it had stood. ... There was a

tall red chimney nearby. Black smoke seemed to
cloud the surface of the Mirror.

It was also during Ronald's time living in Sarehole and
playing in the flat meadows alongside the banks of the River
Cole that he began to have a strange, recurring dream. In it a
great wave would rise up and pour over the fields and forests,
completely covering them. This dream, which Tolkien referred
to as his Atlantis Complex, would trouble him throughout his
life. "It always ends by surrender," Tolkien later explained. "I
wake gasping out of deep water."

The great wave from Tolkien's childhood in Sarehole
would find its way into *The Lord of the Rings* as the fictional
account of the destruction of Numenor, and Faramir's dreams,
like those of his creator, would be haunted by this same vision. At the climactic moment just before the defeat of Sauron,
Tolkien describes Faramir standing with Eowyn on the walls
of Gondor. As they look out into the distance, Faramir tells
her that he is reminded of a "great dark wave climbing over the
green lands and above the hills, and coming on, darkness un-
escapable." And then, surprised that he has broken his silence
and spoken about it, Faramir also confesses: "I often dream of
it."

The house at Number 5 Gracewell Road that served as the
Tolkiens' first home in England is still standing. Given a new

address, Number 264 Wake Green Road also has been given a new purpose. Retaining the old road name, it is now a part of Gracewell Homes, a cluster of retirement residences. Its exterior has not changed much since the time when Mabel and her two young sons lived there. But except for the old mill, which has been preserved, the rural hamlet where Ronald and Hilary romped and played is gone, and in its place is a residential suburb.

The Tolkiens lived in Sarehole for four years. During this period—from the time Ronald was four until he was eight—both he and Hilary were taught at home by their mother. Ronald proved an apt pupil, quickly learning to read and write and developing a passion for drawing and lettering that stayed with him all his life.

Ronald also showed a remarkable skill in language learning, but only when the language appealed to him—a trait that would be characteristic of him. When passionate for a subject, he would display signs of genius. When uninterested, he would be lazy and undisciplined. Ronald learned enough Latin and German from his mother to later be awarded a scholarship to the best private school in Birmingham, but he proved resistant to French. He was equally unaffected by the piano lessons Mabel gave the boys. Later Tolkien would explain to the *Daily Telegraph*: "My interest in languages was derived solely from my mother.... She was also interested in etymology, and aroused my interest in this; and also in alphabets and handwriting."

In addition to their school lessons, Mabel also provided her sons with plenty of books to read. Ronald was especially fond of *The Princess and Curdie* by George MacDonald, as well as *The Story of Sigurd* by Andrew Lang, which tells how the legendary hero of Norse mythology slew the great dragon Fafnir. Later in his famous essay "On Fairy-Stories," Tolkien would recall the yearning that had been brought to life by the books of his childhood. "I desired dragons with a profound desire," he writes, adding: "Of course, I in my timid body did not wish to have them in the neighborhood."

In a letter written to the poet W. H. Auden in 1955, Tolkien reported that he first tried to write a story when he was about seven and chose to write about a dragon. "I remember nothing about it except a philological fact," Tolkien explained. "My mother said nothing about the dragon, but pointed out that one could not say *a green great dragon,* but had to say *a great green dragon.*" Tolkien went on to point out three effects that childhood lessons from his mother had on him, stating, "It has been always with me: the sensibility to linguistic pattern, which affects me emotionally like color or music; the passionate love of growing things; and the deep response to legends."

15

A New School, a New Faith, and a Second Great Loss

Given their lack of money, Mabel knew that her son's only chance of obtaining a university education would be to win a scholarship. And to win a university scholarship, Ronald would have to be taught at the best and most selective private school in Birmingham: King Edward's. With this in mind, Mabel arranged for him to take the entrance exam, and in September 1900, at the age of eight and a half, Ronald was admitted to begin classes. Although two years later he would be awarded a Foundation Scholarship, initially his tuition of £12 per year was paid for by one of Arthur's brothers.

Founded in 1552 by Royal Charter of King Edward VI, the son of Henry VIII and Jane Seymour, King Edward's School was located near the center of Birmingham. For the first weeks Ronald walked several miles each day to catch the tram into the city. There was a train station nearer Sarehole, but trains were too expensive. Realizing that her son could not continue making such a long journey, Mabel decided to pack up the family and move closer in, thus ending the four years of paradise Ronald had enjoyed. "Four years," Tolkien would later write, "but the longest-seeming and most formative part of my life."

Mabel and her two sons lived in a series of dreary apartments in Birmingham—which in 1900 was a city of half a million plagued by poverty and rapid industrialization. For Ronald, the only plus was that one of the apartments backed onto a railroad yard, and he delighted in the mysterious, unpronounceable names on the Welsh coal cars that rumbled in and out from such exotic destinations as *Nantyglo* and *Penrhiwceiber*.

Though he would not learn Welsh until after he became a student at Oxford, Tolkien's boyhood delight in the language never left him. Tolkien later described how as a young person Welsh had come to him "out of the west" and had intrigued him as a language that was "old and yet alive." He also noted that many of the names of the people and places in *The Lord of the Rings* were composed on patterns deliberately modeled on those of Welsh. In addition, Tolkien would later turn to Welsh for the sounds and grammar of Sindarin, one of two languages spoken by his Elves.

Around the same time that Mabel moved with her two boys to be closer to King Edward's, she made another, even greater change in her life. In June 1900, leaving behind the church in which she and Arthur had been married and their children had been christened, Mabel Tolkien was received into the Roman Catholic Church. What is more, she began to instruct her two sons in the Catholic faith. Her actions immediately were met with hostility from her Protestant relatives on both sides of the family—and not just hostility, but the loss of their financial support as well.

While Mabel's embrace of the Catholic faith was a major step in her life and the life of her sons, there is very little record of exactly what it was that caused her to convert. We do know that the young widow facing life alone with two young sons turned to her faith more and more for consolation, and that initially she found solace for her difficulties by attending a high Anglican church where the ritual practices were closer to those of Roman Catholicism. The move from this Anglo-Catholic church to Catholicism was a step further in the direction she had been heading.

In 1953 Tolkien wrote to a friend expressing gratitude for "having been brought up (since I was eight) in a Faith that had nourished me and taught me all the little that I know." Might Tolkien's use of the phrase *since I was eight* mean that prior to that time, his Christian upbringing was in some way absent or lacking?

Perhaps. We find further support for this position in a letter Tolkien wrote in 1965, where he gives us another small window into his early religious upbringing. There he writes about the influence that his guardian, Father Francis, had on him, stating: "I first learned charity and forgiveness from him." Then Tolkien goes on to add: "It pierced even the 'liberal' darkness out of which I came."

In December 1903, Mabel wrote to her mother-in-law with news of a big event in Ronald's spiritual life, and in her announcement we can hear echoes of the antagonism she had faced following her conversion. "My dear Mrs. Tolkien," Mabel begins, and then talks about the boys' drawings that she has included with the letter. It is only in the very last two sentences that she adds: "Ronald is making his First Communion this Christmas—so it is a very great feast indeed to us this year. I don't say this to vex you—only you say you like to know everything about them." In her closing we can hear hopes for a reconciliation, as she signs it: "Yours always lovingly, Mab."

Whatever the reasons for Mabel's conversion, Ronald's new faith would serve him well throughout his life. Biographer Joseph Pearce makes the point that it was because of his deep and abiding faith that Tolkien was able to accept the sorrows of life with patient forbearance and notes that even "his distressed disapproval of the way society was 'progressing' was tempered by sincere hope in the grace of God."

Ronald had been four when his father died. He was eight when his mother became a Catholic and was ostracized by both sides of the family. When he was twelve, he and his younger brother suffered yet another great blow, this one even more devastating. On November 14, 1904, Mabel Tolkien died of complications resulting from Type 1 Diabetes—two decades before the insulin treatment we know today would become available. She was thirty-four.

Exactly what the childhood loss of a mother has to do with

writing extraordinarily captivating and heartrending fantasy literature later in life can only be speculated, but it seems something more than coincidence that it was a loss three of the world's greatest fantasy authors each suffered. C. S. Lewis, who would become Tolkien's close friend and supporter, was nine when his mother died. George MacDonald, whose writings had a major impact on both Tolkien and Lewis, lost his mother when he was eight.

Motherless characters would be even more numerous in Tolkien's fiction than fatherless ones—among them we find Sam, Boromir and Faramir, and Eowyn and Eomer. In addition, Arwen and her two brothers are without a mother, as Celebrian has left Middle-earth and passed over the sea to the Blessed Realm. Most significantly in the family tree found in the appendices at the end of *The Lord of the Rings*, we learn that Frodo was twelve when his parents died in a boating accident, leaving him an orphan at exactly the age Ronald was when he lost his only surviving parent.

Later in life, Tolkien wrote that with the death of his mother, he felt like "a castaway left on a barren island under a heedless sky after the loss of a great ship." C. S. Lewis turned to a similar metaphor to describe his own loss, writing: "With my mother's death all settled happiness, all that was tranquil and reliable, disappeared from my life. There was to be much fun, many pleasures, many stabs of Joy; but no more of the old security. It was sea and islands now; the great continent had sunk like Atlantis."

King Edward's and First Love

When Mabel saw death was approaching, rather than entrusting Ronald and Hilary to the care of their grandparents, she designated Father Francis Morgan, their firm but friendly parish priest at the Birmingham Oratory, to be the boys' legal guardian, knowing this would ensure they would continue to be raised Catholic. Even apart from Mabel's religious considerations, it was a wise choice, for Father Francis would display not only great affection for the Tolkien brothers but also unfailing generosity. Mabel and Arthur had left behind only £800 in investments. Over the years, Father Francis, who had income from a business that belonged to his family, would add to this amount with money of his own to provide for his two wards.

For a brief time there was a possibility that Mabel's will would be contested by her family and the boys would be sent off to a Protestant boarding school. But a compromise of sorts seems to have been reached. In January 1905, Ronald and Hilary—now ages thirteen and eleven—still under the guardianship of Father Francis, went to stay with their Aunt Beatrice, the widow of Mabel's youngest brother, William. Auntie Bea, as the boys called her, had no strong views on religion and being a widow was also in need of money and happened to have an upstairs bedroom to let.

Beatrice Suffield also lived close to the Oratory, and this proved fortunate, for it soon became clear that while she could offer her two nephews room and board, she had little affection to give them. And so it was the Oratory that became Ronald and Hilary's real home during this time. The boys would rise early in the morning and serve as altar boys for Father Francis. After Mass they would eat breakfast with the priests in the refectory before heading off to King Edward's together.

Founded by the son of Henry VIII, King Edward's was and always had been a Protestant school. Looking back at this time in a letter to his son, Michael, Tolkien recalled how he had the advantages of both a first-rate school in King Edward's and—referring to the Oratory where the priests had made him feel like a junior member—a "good Catholic home." Tolkien did not see growing up in this "two-front" situation, as he put it, to be a problem, and pointed out that he took no harm from any of his studies under his Protestant teachers at school, specifically mentioning the New Testament class taught by the headmaster. In fact, Tolkien concluded, his time at King Edward's made him better equipped to make his way in the non-Catholic professional society he later found at Oxford.

At King Edward's, Ronald soon made a best friend. Christopher Wiseman came from a family of staunch Methodists, and Tolkien would later characterize his father as "one of the most delightful Christian men" he had ever met. The two boys shared a love of ancient languages as well as a good-natured academic rivalry—each causing the other to try harder than he might have otherwise. At the end of autumn term 1905, Ronald was ranked first in their class and Christopher second. The two boys also shared a love of rugby and played on the same house team, with Tolkien being made captain during his senior year.

Besides a love of the classical languages, which were part of the core curriculum in English schools at this time, Ronald also developed a passion for Old and Middle English and a determination to master the languages in which *Beowulf* and Chaucer's *Canterbury Tales* had been written. Later he would state that he took to Middle English the moment he set eyes on it as though it was a "known tongue" to him. Besides learning other languages, Ronald was also beginning to invent his own, a practice that would culminate later in his creation of the languages of Middle-earth.

Although his first academic posting at Oxford would be as a Professor of Anglo-Saxon, a better word for Tolkien's

future profession is *philologist*, someone who loves words—
their origins, meanings, and historical development, as well as
the rules that govern them. Later in life he commented: "I am
a pure philologist. I like history, and am moved by it, but its
finest moments for me are those in which it throws light on
words and names."

During the time Ronald was going to classes at King Edward's, playing rugby, and enjoying learning new languages,
there was another strand to his life that no one knew about—
not his school chums, not his teachers, and most important,
not Father Francis. What was this great secret no one could
know about?

Ronald had fallen in love.

Late in 1907, after learning that his two wards were un-
happy living with their emotionally distant aunt, Father Francis had begun to hunt for more congenial lodgings. Not far
from the Oratory, he knew of a wine merchant and his wife
who took in boarders. He had been to many pleasant musical evenings hosted by Mrs. Faulkner, and felt confident she
could provide Ronald and Hilary with supervision that was
both firm and affectionate. Near the start of 1908, he arranged
for the boys to move into their new room on the second floor of
37 Duchess Road. Ronald had just turned sixteen.

Also living at Duchess Road was a young woman who often played piano at Mrs. Faulkner's musical soirees. Although

she was nineteen, and thus three years older than Ronald, pictures from the time reveal her as looking a good deal younger. What is more, she had lost both her mother and her father and, like the Tolkien brothers, was all alone in the world. Her name was Edith Bratt. She would be Tolkien's first love and his last.

Eight years later—after a rocky courtship, three years of forced separation, and a two-year engagement—Edith Bratt would become Edith Tolkien. And though the two would remain married until Edith's death fifty-five years later, early on the young couple must have believed they were star-crossed and any chance of romance between them was doomed.

The difficulties that arose early in the courtship suggest that had everyone—Ronald, Edith, and Father Francis—all shown a little more patience and good sense, a good deal of the pain that ensued could have been avoided. The facts, as we know them, are these.

Within the first few months after Ronald and Hilary moved to Duchess Road, Edith formed not only a friendship with the Tolkien brothers but an alliance. Without the knowledge of the "Old Lady," as they called Mrs. Faulkner, and assisted by Annie Gollins, the Faulkners' maid, Edith found a way to smuggle extra food up to the new boys by means of a basket that they lowered from their window to hers. At other times when they were certain Mrs. Faulkner was out, the three met for secret feasts in Edith's room. Soon Ronald and Edith developed a special whistle they used to summon the other to the window. In a letter written to Edith long afterwards, Tolkien would fondly remember their "absurd long window talks" that lasted well into the night while off in the distance the bell in the Birmingham clock tower tolled away the hours.

By the end of the brothers' first year at Mrs. Faulkner's, Ronald and Edith were secretly meeting in Birmingham tea-shops and taking clandestine bicycle rides together. Six months later, in the summer of 1909, Edith and Ronald decided they were in love.

In autumn term of 1909, Ronald and Edith took a bike ride one afternoon to the Lickey Hills, a scenic area about ten miles southwest of the Birmingham city center. As always, they were careful to leave and return separately, but this time the couple was noticed having tea together. When news of the rendezvous reached Father Francis, he demanded that Ronald end the romantic relationship immediately.

By today's standards his response may seem rash, an over-reaction at best and uncompassionate at worst. And yet Father Francis was not someone prone to overreacting or making rash decisions, nor was he without real affection for the bookish teenager he had promised to care for. Several issues factored in to his decision.

First, Edith was three years older than Ronald. Second, she was a Protestant. A century ago, not just Father Francis, but society in general would have viewed a seventeen-year-old boy dating a twenty-year-old woman and a courtship outside of one's faith with serious misgivings. Third, in a time when proper dating was chaperoned or supervised in some way, the couple had met secretly behind the backs of their guardians and had lied about their real activities.

Fourth, and perhaps most important, in less than two months Ronald would go to Oxford to take the all-important scholarship exam—and a scholarship was absolutely necessary if he was to continue his education. Father Francis was concerned that the seventeen-year-old high school student was not devoting sufficient time studying for the test—and as it turned out, rightly so. Though all of his teachers thought him bright enough, Ronald failed to win a scholarship in December 1909. He would have one last chance to try a year later.

Father Francis moved the Tolkiens to new lodgings, and Ronald and Edith, for the most part, put their relationship on hold. But a month later, in January 1910, they decided to meet for tea—without first asking permission—to celebrate her twenty-first birthday. Once more they were found out. And now the eighteen-year-old Ronald was forbidden by his guardian from having any contact with Edith until he came of age three years later.

Much later in a letter to his oldest son, Michael, Tolkien attempted to give some advice on the subject of marriage and

27

confessed that his own early decisions involving Michael's mother had been "imprudent in nearly every point" so that finally he was faced with two bad choices: either to disobey and deceive the guardian who had been like a father to him or to end the love affair until he turned twenty-one. He chose the latter.

In March 1910, Edith moved from Birmingham to Cheltenham. Now age twenty-one, Edith had accepted the invitation to live with Mr. and Mrs. Jessop, two elderly family friends. While it was a distance of only fifty miles, to the young couple it must have seemed like many more. By chance, Ronald had one last bittersweet glimpse of Edith as she was leaving for the train station. Though distraught, Ronald wrote "Thank, God" in his diary, for it seemed like the best possible solution—for now.

THE T.C.B.S. AND LEAVING THE NEST

After Edith left Birmingham, Ronald had nine months to get ready for his second and final try for an Oxford scholarship. Again his preparation for the exam proved less-than-adequate. On December 17, 1910, he learned he had not done well enough to be given a scholarship but had earned a lesser award, an Exhibition in Classics to Exeter College.

The Exhibition would provide £60 per year. This along

with a small school-leaving scholarship from King Edward's and some extra funds from Father Francis would make it possible for Ronald to attend Oxford—if he was careful about his spending. With his romance with Edith on hold and his academic future now at least partially secure, Ronald set out to enjoy his last two terms at King Edward's.

"I ought to have got a good scholarship," Tolkien would later confess. "I was clever, but not industrious or single-minded." A large part of his failure, he explained, was time that should have been devoted to studying for the exam was often spent studying something else—including a great deal of time on languages such as Old English, Finnish, and Gothic that he would not be tested over. This habit of studying something other than what he was supposed to study would follow Ronald to Oxford and affect his major field of study there.

During the time Ronald was supposed to be studying for the scholarship exam, he was also often guilty of *doing* something else. Besides rugby, he was active in King Edward's Debating Society—where he spoke with great enthusiasm, if not always great enunciation, already displaying the rapid, indistinct style of speech that would be characteristic of him. He had a gift for delivering lengthy orations not only in English but, when the topic called for it, also in Latin, Greek, Gothic, or Anglo-Saxon. In the pre-war England of 1910, Officer Training Corps had sprung up at many schools. Ronald took

TOLKIEN

further time away from potential studying to train with the unit at King Edward's and was chosen to be one of eight cadets from his school who lined the Buckingham Palace parade route in June 1911 as George V ascended the throne. Later at Oxford before his enlistment, he would train with a cavalry regiment where he gained a great deal of experience handling horses—experience that would be put to good use in describing the Riders of Rohan in *The Lord of the Rings*.

At King Edward's, as at most private schools in Britain, a number of administrative duties were carried out by the older boys and prefects. Because of his keen interest in books, Ronald was given the title of librarian during his senior year and quickly recruited his friend Christopher Wiseman to assist him. What happened next would play a key role in Tolkien's development as a writer.

As Wiseman later explained, exams were given during summer term and went on for weeks. In between tests with little to do, Tolkien and Wiseman began hosting private teas in a hidden library cubbyhole. Though in direct violation of school rules, the boys were not overly concerned about being caught because Rob Gilson, the headmaster's son, was part of their illicit gatherings. A number of different students attended the Tea Club, but four members made up its unofficial core: Tolkien, Wiseman, Gilson, and G. B. Smith. While having tea and eating smuggled in food—which they referred to as *subventions*—initially formed the basis for the illicit meetings, gradually discussion and recitations from epic literature and their own written works took center stage.

When the term ended and with it Tolkien's post as librarian, the Tea Club gatherings were moved down the street to the tearoom of a Birmingham department store named Barrow's. Thus, in the summer of 1911, the Tea Club, Barrovian Society—or T.C.B.S.—was officially created. Though later at Oxford Tolkien would be a member of the *Coalbiters*, a group that met to read Icelandic sagas, and after that would be a part of the far more famous *Inklings*, the group that included C. S. Lewis and out of which would come some of the greatest fantasy literature the world had ever seen—it would be at these meetings of the Tea Club, Barrovian Society that young Ronald Tolkien first discovered that he should and could become a writer.

Ronald's final term at King Edward's came to an end on July 26, 1911, with the school's annual Speech Day—a day of prize-giving and musical and dramatic productions, which that year included a performance of "The Peace," by Aristophanes, with Tolkien playing the part of Hermes. In the eleven years since Ronald had taken his first class there, much had happened: he and Hilary had moved a number of times, his mother had died, he had started a romance and then had to break it off, and he had won an Exhibition to Oxford. He also had developed a near kinship with the other three members of the T.C.B.S. These ties, along with the superb linguistic skills he had developed, would accompany him to university.

A few weeks after graduation, Ronald went with a group of family friends on a holiday to the Swiss Alps. Like his experiences during the time he lived at Sarehole, this trip would live on in his memory and have an influence on his writing.

In 1967, Tolkien's son Michael would visit the same region his father had hiked in fifty-six years earlier. "I am delighted that you have made the acquaintances of Switzerland," Tolkien wrote in a letter, "and of the very part that I once knew best and which had the deepest effect on me." He then went on to share his recollections of how their party—which had included Michael's Uncle Hilary—had travelled on foot carrying great packs through the mountain paths.

At one point the group was strung out in a line along a narrow track crossing a glacier, with a sheer drop down a ravine on their left and a steep snow slope on their right. Suddenly an avalanche of rocks, freed from the melting summer ice, came crashing down on the path and plunged into the chasm below. Even though he nearly perished in the rock slide, Tolkien told his son that the trip had been a remarkable experience after his "poor boy's childhood" and stated that Bilbo's journey from Rivendell to the other side of the Misty Mountains, and particularly the company's slide down the avalanche of stones into the pine woods, had been based on his hiking adventures in 1911.

During the holiday, Ronald made a drawing in his sketchbook with the title "The Misty Mountains," a name he later would give to the range that both Bilbo and Frodo must cross on their quests. Some time after he got back to England, Ronald purchased a postcard of the painting by the German artist Josef Madlener titled *Der Berggeist*, "The Mountain Spirit," which reminded him of his trek in the Alps. Madlener's picture shows an old man with a white beard sitting on a large rock beneath an ancient pine tree. Wearing a round, wide-brimmed hat and a long cloak, the old man seems to be saying something to the strange white deer that is nuzzling his hand. Off on the horizon, a distant range of mountains can be seen. On the paper cover that Tolkien would keep the postcard in, he would later write "Origin of Gandalf."

In the opening chapter of *The Fellowship of the Rings*, Bilbo says to Gandalf, "I want to see mountains again, Gandalf—*mountains*." It would be a statement expressed often by Tolkien himself in his later years as he looked back on the trip he made in the summer of 1911 between leaving King Edward's and beginning at Exeter.

Soon not only the summer holidays but also Tolkien's boyhood life in Birmingham came to a close, and with it the fun times with the close friends he loved. It was time to leave and enter a larger world. "I felt," Tolkien later confessed, "like a young sparrow kicked out of a high nest."

PART TWO
SCHOLAR AND SOLDIER

EXETER COLLEGE STUDENT

Founded in 1314, Exeter is the fourth-oldest of the thirty-eight individual colleges that make up Oxford University. Visitors today to its beautiful Victorian chapel will find a striking bust of Tolkien on prominent display near the entrance. Cast in bronze from the plaster version made by Faith Tolkien, the author's daughter-in-law, and lit from above by dramatic lighting, the installation is a fitting tribute to Exeter's most famous son.

But for the first half of his undergraduate career, there was little evidence that J. R. R. Tolkien would one day be numbered among the college's most accomplished and revered alumni. In fact, most of the evidence suggested that something more the opposite would be true.

Divided into three eight-week terms, each named for a feast in the church calendar, the academic year at Oxford is slightly different from the American semester system. The year starts in mid-October with Michaelmas, named for the Mass or Feast of St. Michael. This term lasts through the first week in December. Hilary, so called because the feast of St. Hilary falls during this term, begins in mid-January and finishes in mid-March. Trinity term gets its name from Trinity Sunday and begins near the end of April and finishes in mid-June.

On a mid-October day in 1911, Ronald was taken by his former literature teacher, R. W. Reynolds, to begin Michaelmas term at Exeter College. Although the seventy-mile journey was mostly south, whatever direction (or altitude) students depart from, they "come up" to Oxford when they begin and "go down" when they finish—or are "sent down" if expelled. Two aspects of the trip would live on in Tolkien's memory: it was uncommonly hot for an autumn day, and they made the journey by car, which was still quite a novelty at the time. Once at Exeter, Tolkien—as we shall now call him—was shown up to number 9 on the number 7 staircase. With both a sitting room and a bedroom—albeit a small one—a scout to serve him breakfast and tidy up, and a window that looked out onto Turl Street, or "the Turl" as it is called, his new circumstances seemed truly amazing to the young man who had lived most of his life on the south side of Birmingham.

Oxford! For the next four years Tolkien not only would study in the celebrated "city of dreaming spires," but also it would become his home. Six decades earlier, the poet Matthew Arnold had been an Oxford student, and it was he who gave the city its famous epithet. In the poem "Thyrsis," he declares:

And that sweet city with her dreaming spires,
She needs not June for beauty's heightening,
Lovely all times she lies, lovely to-night!

Within the first two weeks after his arrival, Tolkien set out to write his own tribute to his new home. Penned in October 1911 and later published in Exeter's *Stapledon Magazine*, Tolkien's poem "From Iffley" describes the view of Oxford as seen from Iffley village, just a short walking distance down the Thames:

From the many-willow'd margin of the immemorial Thames,
Standing in a vale outcarven in a world-forgotten day,
There is dimly seen uprising through the greenly veiled stems,
Many-mansion'd, tower-crowned in its dreamy robe of grey,
All the city by the fording: aged in the lives of men,
Proudly wrapt in mystic mem'ry overpassing human ken.

A *tower-crowned* city that is *aged in lives of men* and wrapped in a *mystic memory* that goes beyond *human ken* or knowledge. Already in the nineteen-year-old's writing we see aspects that would appear in his later work: the elevated tone, his inclination for ancient words with mysterious undertones, his ability to suggest something hidden beneath the surface. Here we also are given, as biographer John Garth points out, "an early glimpse of the spirit of place" that would pervade all of Tolkien's fiction.

Tolkien scholar Tom Shippey has observed that while "From Iffley" describes Oxford, it could well be read as a fitting description for Gondor and its ancient city of Minas Tirith to which Aragorn, its long-lost king, yearns to return. In *The Two Towers*, as the sun rises to reveal the distant ramparts, Tolkien has Aragorn cry out:

> *Gondor! Gondor, between the Mountains and the Sea!*
> *West Wind blew there; the light upon the Silver Tree*
> *Fell like bright rain in gardens of the Kings of old.*
> *O proud walls! White towers! O wingéd crown and throne*
>   *of gold!*

In British universities more so than in American, students come in already having declared their major. Tolkien was admitted to "read" Classics—which consisted of mostly Greek and Latin literature but also some philosophy and classical history. British universities also have far fewer and hence far more important tests. Tolkien's first major exam would be Honor Moderations, which he would "sit for" after his first eighteen months. A second and final set of major tests, called Schools, would come at the completion of his four years of study.

Looking back on his first terms at Oxford, Tolkien later would confess that he soon fell back into the same "folly and slackness" that had characterized much of his time at King

Edward's. In fact, it was not simply slackness that was the problem. Despite lectures to attend, a large amount of required reading to do, and weekly tutorials to prepare where he would meet one-on-one with his tutor and read out an essay he had written, Tolkien also devoted a great deal of his time and energy to a wide range of nonacademic university activities. He was always quite ready to be a part of the general, undergraduate, male boisterousness—or "festivity" as he called it. In addition, Tolkien continued to play rugby, though not on the college team, and was active in the college's Essay Club, the Dialectical Society, and the Stapeldon—the debating society named after Walter de Stapeldon, Bishop of Exeter, who had founded the college.

In the tradition of the T.C.B.S., Tolkien also started his own club, the Apolausticks (which later gave way to the Chequers Clubbe), whose members held discussions, engaged in debates, and put on dinners—though much more elaborate ones than those smuggled into the King Edward's library or eaten in the Barrow's Stores café.

Five weeks into Tolkien's first term, on November 25, 1911, Exeter Library records indicate that he checked out *A Finnish Grammar*, by Charles Eliot, a pioneering work published only two decades earlier. He was not taking a class that required Finnish. This was simply a subject that interested him.

"My object in writing this book has been to give an account of Finnish sufficient to enable anyone to understand the grammatical structure of the written language," Eliot begins, "and also to place before the student of philology an account of the chief phenomena it presents."

While it may be hard for modern readers to imagine the fire that these opening words ignited inside the young Oxford freshman, Tolkien later confessed that the new language intoxicated him and compared the experience to discovering a wine cellar filled with bottles of "an amazing wine of a kind and flavor never tasted before." Consequently he spent many hours, hours that should have been spent on his exam subjects, teaching himself Finnish, and through its inspiration he began to develop Quenya, the language that his High Elves would speak.

Back when he was a student at King Edward's, Tolkien had discovered a mediocre English translation of the *Kalevala*, the collection of ancient Finnish songs and stories that had been compiled and arranged in the nineteenth century by country doctor and amateur philologist Elias Lonnrot. Now, gradually, he was able to read the Finns' great national epic in its original language.

Tolkien later would state that there was "something in the air" of the *Kalevala* that was immensely attractive, something which, as he put it, set off a rocket in him. Over the coming

years, it would spark a desire in Tolkien to create a similar mythology for England, which he believed had lost much of its
ancient folklore after the Norman Invasion of 1066. In an essay
written during his time at Exeter about the importance of the
kind of mythology found in the Finnish poems, he lamented:
"I would that we had more of it left—something of the same
sort that belonged to the English." In a letter to W. H. Auden,
he would later explain that the beginning of his *legendarium*—
Tolkien's term for his three great works set in Middle-earth:
The Silmarillion, The Hobbit, and *The Lord of the Rings*—all
began as an attempt to reorganize some of the *Kalevala* into a
form of his own.

At Oxford, Tolkien also further developed his skills in
painting and drawing, and he began to show genuine aptitude
in both these areas, especially in his landscape sketches. He
continued his interest in handwriting and calligraphy as well,
and became proficient in many different styles of script. One
of his drawings during this time would be chosen for the program cover of the November 19, 1913 *Exeter College Smoker,*
a college concert. The picture shows four festive and apparently inebriated young scholars in evening dress winding their
way down Turl Street smoking pipes. Four owls, dressed to
represent school officials, circle above the students, watching
in disapproval. And if we look closely in the lower left-hand
corner, we can see that even at this early point in his career,

Tolkien was signing his drawings with the distinctive *JRRT* monogram he would use throughout his life.

On February 27, 1913—a year and a half into his studies—Tolkien sat for his Honor Moderations where students may pass with a First, Second, or Third. A First was certainly within his capabilities and was expected of anyone who intended to pursue an academic career as Tolkien now did. Students majoring in Classics were required to produce a series of twelve papers or translations covering a wide range of Greek and Latin literature. With a particularly dismal score for his translation of Virgil and his paper on Tacitus, Tolkien barely scraped by with a Second, and might even have sunk to a Third, except for the fact that he earned an "alpha"—or perfect score—on his Comparative Philology Paper. He would later confess, "Finnish nearly ruined my Honor Mods."

In fact, Finnish, combined with Tolkien's many other interests not related to the Classics, nearly ruined not just his Honor Mods, but his entire Oxford career. In 1955 he would write Auden, "I came very near having my Exhibition taken off me if not being sent down." And here again in Tolkien's life we find someone stepping in and playing an important role in what was to come.

Lewis Farnell, who had been Tolkien's Classics tutor, realized that his young charge had enormous potential but only if permitted to follow his passion—which, it was clear, had something to do with the philology of ancient Germanic languages, not Greek or Latin. So rather than taking Tolkien's dismal performance personally, Farnell worked behind the scenes to allow Tolkien not only to change to the English School, with its emphasis then on Old and Middle English, but also to keep the Exhibition that had originally been intended to fund his studies in Classics. In an interesting twist, it was only quite late in life after Tolkien was a professor himself that he learned of the kind actions his tutor had taken on his behalf.

And so, in the Trinity term of 1913, John Ronald Tolkien left Greek and Latin behind and began what would become his lifelong professional career in English (especially Old and Middle English) language and literature. Though it may seem surprising today, Oxford had only recently acquired an English School, the equivalent of an English Department in the States. Founded in 1894, the program was in its early stages when Tolkien joined it in 1913, which partly may explain why he was not an English major from the start. In fact, he would later state that he only discovered its existence while browsing the Examination Statutes.

Knowing that there were some who questioned the need for an English degree—since English seemed to be something that anyone could read without needing to study it—the Oxford School of English Language and Literature was deliberately weighed more heavily on philological science than on literary interpretation. And this perfectly suited the young Tolkien, who loved the study of words and had no taste for modern writers—which for him meant no writer later than Chaucer.

Finally the subjects Tolkien was passionate about and the subjects he was required to study had come together. It was another great turning point in his life.

Reunion with Edith and The Council of London

When it had come to studying for his Honor Mods, there had been a further distraction for Tolkien in addition to his many non-exam interests and his robust enjoyment of Oxford's social life. This distraction was due to the fact that his twenty-first birthday came seven weeks before he needed to be ready for his tests. At one second past midnight on January 3, 1913, in the first moments after he came of age, Tolkien ended the long, agreed-upon three-year silence and began a letter to Edith.

His feelings toward her had not changed. If anything, his love had grown stronger during their separation. Now legally an adult and having fulfilled Father Francis's decree, all Tolkien was interested in was knowing her answer to one question. How long would it be, he wrote, before they could be joined together before God and the world?

Several days later, Tolkien received a letter posted from Cheltenham in a hand he still recognized. In it Edith replied that after leaving Birmingham she had felt like she had been put on the shelf and was afraid she might be left there, a growing concern since she was now almost twenty-four—an age when most women in 1913 were already married. Over the months and years with no contact, she had struggled to believe that he still cared for her and would want to see her. In the meantime a local young man, the brother of a friend, had been kind to her—extremely so. This kind young man, a farmer named George Field, had asked her to marry him. She had agreed, and they were now engaged.

Hearing hints in her letter that she might be open to persuasion now that he had reaffirmed his love, Tolkien wrote again, and a meeting was arranged. On January 8, Tolkien took the train to Cheltenham where he found Edith waiting at the station. The young couple took a long walk out into the countryside where they sat together beneath a railway viaduct and opened their hearts to each other. The end result was that Edith agreed to marry him, though for the time being they decided to keep their engagement a secret, and the hapless George Field was given his ring back.

The reason they decided to keep their betrothal a secret was the fact that Tolkien was still a very poor scholar, and it was unclear what his prospects would be and how he might support a wife and any children they might have. Though he felt remorse for their earlier duplicity, Tolkien said nothing to Father Francis about his reunion with Edith and would choose to wait until the last minute to inform him that he and Edith planned to marry. Perhaps he feared further disapproval from the man who had been like a father to him. In addition, though Tolkien was now legally of age, he was still dependent on Father Francis to help pay for his remaining two years at Oxford. He may have feared this support would be withdrawn if news of their engagement reached his former guardian.

With his poor performance on his Honor Mods now behind him and a new field of study he was better suited for ahead of him, Tolkien promised Edith he would work more dutifully to earn the kind of degree that could ensure an academic posting and a future for the two of them. He began a diary in which he kept a record of the number of hours he worked on his studies. He also became more serious about attending mass and keeping his religious duties—for he had allowed these responsibilities to slip as well during his first terms at Exeter.

In addition to needing to do exceptionally well on his final exams and then to secure an academic position, there was a further obstacle to Ronald and Edith becoming married. For their marriage to be blessed by the Catholic Church, something Tolkien insisted upon, Edith would have to convert. While Edith did not have any major theological obstacles preventing her from joining the Roman Catholic Church, she did have two social ones. First, during their three years apart, she had been quite active and popular in her local Anglican church in Cheltenham where she served as the organist for services. Leaving the church that had become a home for her would be difficult.

Second, Edith believed that as soon as she announced her intentions to become a Catholic she no longer would be welcome in the home of the strongly Protestant family friends who had taken her in. In this she was right. The Jessops told her that if she was going to convert, she would have to leave their house at the earliest opportunity. In addition, Mr. Jessop felt it his duty to write Stephen Gateley, the Bratt family lawyer who had been Edith's guardian, to express his misgivings about her husband-to-be.

"I have nothing to say against Tolkien," wrote Jessop, "he is a cultured gentleman, but his prospects are poor in the extreme, and when he will be in a position to marry I cannot imagine. Had he adopted a profession it would have been different."

Had he adopted a profession it would have been different. Jessop can perhaps be forgiven for thinking Edith should have stuck with George Field, who at least had his farm. At this point in 1913, the twenty-one-year-old Tolkien was not even showing signs he would graduate with honors, let alone be able to obtain a competitive academic appointment. It is doubly ironic, then, that Tolkien would be awarded not one, but three successive professor's chairs—in 1924, 1925, and 1945, each better-paying than the previous one and the latter two at the world's most prestigious university—making him a highly successful scholar, and that late in life he would become a millionaire several times over for his fiction and would leave an estate to his children that would come to be worth many millions more.

Edith set up home with an older cousin in Warwick where she was instructed in the faith by the local parish priest, Father Murphy. On January 8, 1914, the first anniversary of their reunion, she was received into the Roman Catholic Church, and she and Tolkien became officially betrothed. For a time, things seemed on track—for graduation, the wedding, and their life afterwards. But on June 28, 1914, a Serbian nationalist killed the Archduke Franz Ferdinand of Austria, setting off events that would lead to an international crisis. After Germany's invasion of Belgium, England declared war on August 4, 1914.

World War I—the "War to End All Wars," as it was called—had begun.

When Tolkien returned to Oxford from summer vacation, a large number of his fellow students already had enlisted, and the student population steadily dropped from three thousand to around one thousand. Many of the younger dons and staff had left to join the war as well. Learning of a program that would allow him to drill in the Officers' Training Corps while remaining at the university, Tolkien signed on. With his call-up deferred until the following summer after he finished his degree, Tolkien applied himself diligently to his studies.

After Tolkien had graduated from King Edward's, the four friends of the T.C.B.S. had remained in touch through letters and an occasional reunion, and gradually their meetings had taken on additional significance. While in the past they had met to read from favorite ancient texts and talk about ideas from the world of books, they gradually began to see themselves as an artistic brotherhood with common goals, a group that might leave some kind of a mark on the world. With the war and their own survival now in the forefront of their thoughts, these concerns became even more emphatic.

On December 12, 1914, Tolkien, Christopher Wiseman, Rob Gilson, and G. B. Smith met at the Wisemans' new home, and the four core members of the T.C.B.S. held the "Council of London," as they called it. This gathering would mark another major turning point for Tolkien.

No records survive to tell us exactly what happened that weekend as the four, no longer boys but young men, sat around the fire in Christopher Wiseman's room and talked until well into the night. But following the Council of London, two convictions took root in Tolkien, which he expressed in a letter to G. B. Smith some months later. First, he came to see that the group had been granted a "spark of fire" by which they were to kindle a new light in the world, or more accurately, to rekindle an old one. As Tolkien put it, the T.C.B.S. was "destined to testify for God and Truth."

Second, Tolkien described the personal "hope and ambitions" that first became conscious at the Council. There for the first time he saw himself and his writing as somehow "a great instrument in God's hands." With apologies for perhaps sounding arrogant, Tolkien told Smith that this realization actually made him feel humbler, weaker, and poorer. Tolkien confessed that he now believed God might work through his writing to make him, as he told Smith, "a mover, a doer, even an achiever of great things, a beginner at the very least of large things."

This astounding sense of sacred calling would underlie, permeate, and inform the rest of Tolkien's life.

A mover. A doer. An achiever of great things. A great instrument in God's hands. Today, people all around the world whose lives have been touched by Tolkien's fiction would answer— yes, exactly! But at this point in 1914, the twenty-two-year-old had exactly two poems published, both in school literary magazines. It would be twenty-three years before *The Hobbit* would be released by Allen & Unwin, and forty years before the first volume of *The Lord of the Rings* would come out. Along the way, Tolkien's belief that his "stuff," as he called it, could ever be more than just a private hobby would wax and wane. There would be times when he was convinced that he would never finish his great works and would completely give up. But an inner conviction, the memory of the T.C.B.S., a word of encouragement from a friend, or sometimes just sheer determination would always be there to help him start again.

Something hard to describe happened to John Ronald Tolkien at the Council of London on that cold December weekend in 1914. As he explained to Smith, the meeting of the four friends enabled him to find a voice for, as he put it, "all kinds of pent up things." But it was more profound than this. Following the Council, Tolkien simply explained, there was "a tremendous opening up of everything for me." All of his talents, interests, and inclinations had come together. He had found his vocation as a writer of a certain kind of writing.

The first evidence of this *tremendous opening up of everything* was that Tolkien went back to Oxford and began to produce a new kind of poetry—including a new work about a mysterious figure named Eärendil, whose name he had come across in a poem written in the ninth century by the Anglo-Saxon poet Cynewulf. Tolkien's Eärendil would, much later, have a role in *The Lord of the Rings* as the father of Elrond.

This new poetry Tolkien began to write was not very good,

not at first. His T.C.B.S. friends found it too ornate, too hard to follow. Wiseman said it reminded him of a woman who wanted to wear all her jewelry at the same time and advised him not to overdo it so much. But at the same time Wiseman expressed wonder at where all Tolkien's "amazing words" were coming from.

It was a first step in the direction that would put Tolkien on the world stage.

In the weeks and months during which the rest of the world was going to war, Tolkien went to lectures and focused diligently on his schoolwork. Finally the morning of June 10, 1915, arrived, and Tolkien reported at Oxford's Sheldonian Theatre to begin his Schools, the final exams that would determine his future. Two years before, he had disappointed everyone on his Honor Mods. This time he thought he was ready.

Each day for the next five days, Tolkien had one paper at 9:30 a.m. and a second at 2:00 p.m., where he would write either an essay or a translation. His subjects included *Beowulf* and other Old English texts; Middle English texts, including the works of Chaucer; Gothic and Germanic Philology; Shakespeare, and other writers; and Historical English Grammar. The last paper on the afternoon of the fifth day was on the candidate's special subject, which Tolkien had chosen to be Scandinavian philology.

On July 2 the results for the Schools exams were posted in Latin as they had been for centuries. Under *Literis Anglicis Classis I* appeared the name *Tolkien, Joannes R. R.* He had earned a First, the highest degree possible. The next day an announcement of Tolkien's first class honors appeared in the *Times*. He now had the ticket he needed for an academic career—if he could survive the war.

Second Lieutenant Tolkien

Two weeks after learning he had succeeded on his exams, Tolkien was commissioned as a second lieutenant in a battalion known as the Lancashire Fusiliers, and on July 19, 1915, he reported for duty. His first months consisted of tedious training drills and lectures. In a letter he wrote to Edith in November, he described a usual day of standing about, freezing, and then trotting to get warmer so as to freeze again, followed by an hour's worth of practicing bomb throwing, and then standing in icy groups out in the open where they were endlessly talked at.

Eventually Tolkien was placed in the signal corps where his Oxford-trained talents as a philologist were put to use learning how to use handheld flags, Morse code, blinking spotlights, and even carrier pigeons to send messages. Pictures from this time show him in the new uniform he had purchased with the regulation £50 allotment he had received to obtain clothes and his personal supplies. They also show Lieutenant Tolkien sporting a mustache, the only time in his life he would wear facial hair, grown perhaps to make him seem older and more of an authority.

Ten months later, knowing that his posting to the front was coming, Ronald and Edith set a wedding date. In one sense they were certainly ready. He was twenty-four, she was twenty-seven, and they had known each other for eight years. At the same time, for three of those eight years they had no contact, and even after their reunion they had spent relatively little time together. While Tolkien was a student at Oxford, the only time Edith had seen her future husband was in-between semesters and on the occasional weekend. After he graduated and joined the Army, his visits—when he would drive to Warwick, where Edith now lived, on a motorcycle he had purchased with a fellow officer—continued to be sporadic and depended on being able to get several days of leave at one time.

In *The Lord of the Rings*, Faramir and Eowyn have even less time together before their betrothal than Ronald and Edith. In 1963 when a reader wrote to Tolkien commenting on the quickness with which the relationship between the two characters develops, Tolkien wrote back to say that he had found *through his own experience*, feelings and decisions ripened very quickly "during periods of great stress, and especially under the expectation of imminent death."

Ready or not, the couple felt they had put off the wedding as long as they could. Two weeks before they were to be married, Tolkien finally got up the courage to inform Father Francis, who wished them "every blessing and happiness" and offered to perform the ceremony in the Oratory Church in Birmingham. But plans already had been made, and the couple was wed on March 22, 1916, in the Warwick church Edith attended, with Father Murphy presiding.

Two and a half months later, Edith bid a tearful farewell to her husband as he boarded a train that would take him to the coast. There a transport ship was docked that would take him to France where the battle was raging. Like many young wives at the time, Edith had very justified fears she would never see her husband again. "One didn't expect to survive, you know," Tolkien would tell an interviewer years later. "Junior officers were being killed off, a dozen a minute. Parting from my wife then—we were only just married—it was like a death."

On June 6, 1916, his ship landed at Calais, and Second Lieutenant Tolkien was shown to his camp, the staging area before advancing to the front. Next came three weeks of inactivity and anxious waiting before orders came to move with his battalion toward the nearby river valley. On July 1, 1916, one of the bloodiest battles in the history of warfare began. It would come to be known as the Battle of the Somme.

Not part of the initial wave, Tolkien and his company were sent into action on July 14, and at 2:00 a.m. the following morning, they went over the top, leaving the trenches for the No Man's Land between the opposing lines. What once had been trees, grassy meadows, and cornfields had been blasted into a muddy, barren plain. Bloated and decaying corpses and parts of corpses were strewn everywhere, filling the air with a horrible stench. Tolkien later would write of the Dead Marshes that Frodo and Sam must cross on their way to Mordor, where they see the dead faces of those who had been killed in a great battle looking up from dirty pools, and he would explain that this setting owed something to his war experiences.

Though unhurt himself, Tolkien witnessed the slaughter of many of his companions, as the days that followed became a grim cycle of a short rest away from the front, then a return to the trenches, an attack that was mostly ineffective and full of causalities from shelling and heavy German machine gun fire, followed by another period of retreat and rest. Before it ended in November, the Battle of the Somme would claim over one million men missing, dead, or wounded.

In the end, Tolkien would spend relatively little time in action. Four and a half months after he arrived in France, he developed a particularly serious case of trench fever, a highly infectious bacterial disease carried by lice that manifested itself as fever, headaches, muscle pain, and weakness. On October 27, Tolkien was pulled from the front, and the next day he was admitted to the officers' hospital. Ten days later, after failing to improve, he was on a ship back to England. He was taken by train to Birmingham for further convalescence, arriving on November 9, 1916—five months and four days after he and Edith had said their tearful good-byes.

At Birmingham's Southern General Hospital, concern for Tolkien's life was high since a great many deaths during World War I were caused by trench fever and other infections rather than by actual combat itself. As there were no antibiotics in those days, little in the form of direct treatment could be done. With Edith living nearby and able to visit, Tolkien's health improved so that he was out of danger, but always with a relapse. Though eventually he would be sent to Yorkshire to retrain, he would not return to battle. The terror of the trenches was over for him.

Biographer John Garth argues that Tolkien's ill health at this time "almost certainly saved his life," as the men from his battalion of the Lancashire Fusiliers who remained at the front were all eventually wiped out. As Edith wrote her husband during one of his many periods of recurring illness, "Every day in bed means another day in England." And another day in England meant another day *not* in combat.

Like many of his generation who survived the carnage of World War I, Tolkien would say relatively little about his experience. Perhaps the horrors of the battlefield, as much as possible, were best left unspoken. It is telling, then, that one place Tolkien brings up his own war suffering is in the foreword to the second edition of *The Lord of the Rings*. In this prominent and well-known statement of his intentions, Tolkien refutes the claim that the War of the Ring had been based on the events of World War II. To the extent that he drew on his experiences, Tolkien suggests that it was to his memories of World War I that he turned.

"As the years go by," he tells readers, "it seems now often forgotten that to be caught in youth by 1914 was no less hideous an experience than to be involved in 1939 and the following years." And it was not only the experience of the war that was hideous for Tolkien. The consequences were equally devastating, as he concludes: "By 1918 all but one of my close friends were dead."

Rob Gilson had been the first of the T.C.B.S. to die after taking command of his battalion in No Man's Land on the first day of the Battle of the Somme. G. B. Smith died on December 3, 1916, after he was wounded by shrapnel and gangrene set in.

Earlier in the war, Smith had written a letter to Tolkien just as he was about to go out on patrol, telling him:

> My chief consolation is, that if I am scuppered
> tonight . . . there will still be left a member of
> the great T.C.B.S. to voice what I dreamed and
> what we all agreed upon. For the death of one of
> its members cannot, I am determined, dissolve
> the T.C.B.S. . . . May God bless you my dear
> John Ronald and may you say things I have
> tried to say long after I am not there to say them
> if such be my lot.

As Lieutenant Tolkien lay in the Birmingham hospital, he and Christopher Wiseman were all that was left of the T.C.B.S. And since Wiseman was not a poet or a writer, Tolkien was the only member left who might give voice to what they had all dreamed of. If anyone was going to say the things that Smith had tried to say long after he was gone, it would have to be him.

Despite continuing to feel weak and to suffer from headaches and pains in the leg, Tolkien continued to show signs of improvement. As the days turned into weeks, he pondered Smith's words, and ideas that had been disconnected began to coalesce. What would eventually become *The Silmarillion* began to take hold in his imagination.

Later in his famous essay titled "On Fairy-Stories," Tolkien would claim there had been something about the war that had "quickened to full life" his taste for fairy-stories. What exactly it was about the war that had brought this taste for fairy-stories, wakened earlier by his interest in philology, to *full life*, he leaves unspoken. There in the Birmingham hospital, he began to conceive "The Fall of Gondolin," the very first story in what would become part of a larger work he would call "The Book of Lost Tales," which would in turn form *The Silmarillion*.

It was another turning point in Tolkien's life. Long before he would write *The Hobbit* and long before he would write *The Lord of the Rings*, he already had constructed Middle-earth's mythology. If *The Lord of the Rings* tells the story of Middle-earth's Third Age, the twenty-four-year-old Tolkien had started upon a set of stories that would take place in its legendary past.

PART THREE
STORYTELLER AND MYTHMAKER

A Mythology for England

After a number of bouts of ill health, Tolkien was deemed better but still unfit for active service. He was discharged from the hospital in Birmingham on December 8, 1916, and granted a month of leave to further recover. As the war raged for almost two more years—with hostilities ending at eleven o'clock in the morning of the eleventh day of the eleventh month of 1918—Tolkien eventually would return to duty, but he would not leave the country or see combat again. During this time, he would continue to have periods when he would relapse, often requiring further hospitalization and either extended leave from service or at least only light duties.

He also would use this time to work on his stories for *The Book of Lost Tales*.

In 1951, Tolkien wrote a long letter to Milton Waldman, an editor at Collins publishers who had expressed interest in publishing *The Lord of the Rings*. With *The Hobbit* already having published in 1937, Tolkien was hoping to convince Waldman to publish both *The Lord of the Rings* and *The Silmarillion*, his other great work. And so he sent Waldman a lengthy explanation of how *The Lord of the Rings* and *The Silmarillion* were connected and, in Tolkien's mind, indivisible. Although his attempts to convince Waldman to take on *The Silmarillion* were unsuccessful, the letter provides key insights into what Tolkien was attempting to do in the collection of stories he began during his recovery in 1914 and the part they played in the fiction that came afterwards.

"Once upon a time," Tolkien wrote, "I had a mind to make a body of more or less connected legend . . . which I could dedicate simply: to England; my country."

What was it that had prompted this grand desire in Tolkien? "I was from early days," Tolkien explained to Waldman, "grieved by the poverty of my own beloved country." There was Greek and Roman mythology, Celtic mythology, Scandinavian and Finnish mythology, but no real English mythology, Tolkien argued. Even the King Arthur tales had their origins in post–1066 England and so were more connected to Norman and French influences than to British prehistory.

And so after he left the Birmingham hospital, Tolkien purchased a big notebook, took out a thick blue pencil, and on its cover wrote "The Book of Lost Tales" and began to write. Eventually a number of these lost tales would be shaped into *The Silmarillion.*

Along with other stories, *The Silmarillion* would tell the history of the Silmarils, three living and sacred gemstones, fashioned in Middle-earth's First Age by the Elf craftsman Fëanor and stolen from the blessed realm of Valinor by the evil Morgoth. Though *The Silmarillion* would not be accepted by publishers during Tolkien's lifetime, its creation was critical to *The Hobbit* and *The Lord of the Rings* because it supplied the vast historical backdrop against which Tolkien's later works would be set. Because Tolkien had lived in what he called his *secondary world* for decades before writing *The Hobbit* and *The Lord of the Rings*—breathing its air, supplying its languages, and sketching out its history and geography—Middle-earth feels completely real to us when we go there to walk alongside Bilbo and Frodo.

Three specific examples will help illustrate the relationship between Tolkien's less-accessible early stories and his best-selling fiction, which came later. Early in *The Fellowship of the Ring*, Aragorn and the four hobbits are huddled around the campfire on the slopes of Weathertop. Knowing that the Black Riders are nearby, Sam asks Strider, the hobbits' name for Aragorn, to tell them a tale of Elves and the old days that will lighten their hearts, since, as Sam puts it, "The dark seems to press round so close."

"I will tell you the tale of Tinúviel," Aragorn answers. And then he begins to softly chant: "The leaves were long, the grass was green, / The hemlock-umbels tall and fair." It is the story of the Elf-maiden Lúthien Tinúviel and her meeting with Beren, a great but mortal man. As Aragorn recites the ancient lay, readers are transported along with the hobbits to

Middle-earth's ancient past, a past that seems both very mysterious and very real at the same time—mysterious because we are given only hints of it, real because "The Tale of Tinúviel" had been written by Tolkien as a part of *The Book of Lost Tales* and had been revised and perfected over the years since he first wrote it down back in 1917.

Two chapters later, with Aragorn's help the hobbits have managed to make it to Rivendell. There in the Hall of Fire, after Frodo and Bilbo are reunited, Bilbo recites a verse that he has written himself about Elrond's father, Eärendil, another story of Middle-earth's distant past, which Tolkien drew from *The Book of Lost Tales*.

"Eärendil was a mariner that tarried in Avernien," Bilbo sings. "He built a boat of timber felled in Nimbrethil to journey in." Readers at this point have no idea who Eärendil is or where Avernien or Nimbrethil are, and unless they read the appendices at the end of *The Return of the King*, they never will. But Tolkien knew who they were, having worked these things out long before in the years after he returned from the war. And Tolkien's long familiarity with the legendary figures and places that appear here and there offering glimpses into Middle-earth's past imparts something unique to *The Hobbit* and *The Lord of the Rings* without ever distracting us from the main story, for we never question their inclusion. We somehow feel their rightness without fully understanding who they are.

And we could make the same claim for names of people and places Tolkien uses. There is an inexplicable rightness to them. Gandalf, Galadriel, and Gollum; Boromir, Faramir, and Denethor; Aragorn, Arwen, and Elrond; Sauron, Saruman, and Smaug; Gloin, Gimli, and Legolas; Bilbo, Sam, and Frodo; Bag End, Hobbiton, Mordor, and Rivendell—they just seem to fit the people or places they go with and not sound like a gobbledygook of letters that the author threw together at the last minute. As Gandalf tells Bilbo in the opening chapter of *The Hobbit*: "You do know my name, though you don't remember that I belong to it. I am Gandalf and Gandalf means me!"

One part of this *rightness* Tolkien's names have is due to his ear as a linguist—in early drafts Gandalf was called Bladorthin, Smaug was called Pryftan, and Frodo was called Bingo, but these names did not fit their characters and so had to be changed. The other part of this *rightness* is due to that fact that Tolkien took many of his people and place names in *The Hobbit* and *The Lord of the Rings* from one of the stories or languages he had created and had been perfecting for many years.

While elements from *The Book of Lost Tales* appear more often in *The Lord of the Rings*, we can find unexplained allusions to Middle-earth's distant past in *The Hobbit* as well. Early in the story after Gandalf tricks the three trolls into arguing until dawn so that the rising sun turns them into stone, the wizard has Bilbo and the dwarves help him search for their hidden cave, which must be nearby. Among the stolen treasure they find inside are swords of various makes and sizes.

"These look like good blades," Gandalf observes. "They were not made by any troll, nor by any smith among men in these parts and days." Gandalf and Thorin take two particularly beautiful swords with jeweled hilts and mysterious writing on them. Several pages later the company reaches Rivendell, where Elrond, who can read runes of all kinds, examines them and explains: "These are not troll-make. They are old swords, very old swords of the High Elves of the West, my kin. They were made in Gondolin for the Goblin-wars." And so here in chapter 3 of *The Hobbit*, we find a brief unexplained allusion to "The Fall of Gondolin," the very first story Tolkien wrote in the Birmingham hospital.

During this time of illness, recovery, a return to partial or sedentary duties, and then another bout of illness—while all the time writing and rewriting his new mythology for England, Tolkien had one more notable event that occupied his thoughts. On November 16, 1917, Edith gave birth to a son they named John Francis Reuel Tolkien, after both his father and Father Francis, who came to baptize the baby six days later. John Francis Tolkien would go on to follow in the footsteps of both his namesakes and be a practicing Catholic all his life, eventually entering the seminary and becoming a parish priest.

GAINFUL EMPLOYMENT

Though Tolkien would not receive his official discharge from military services until a number of months later, he visited Oxford in October 1918 to inquire about possible teaching openings. Unlike today, at that time graduate degrees were relatively rare, and positions at universities were given often to candidates having only an undergraduate degree. (Further muddling the issue was the fact that Oxford graduates typically were awarded a Master of Arts degree more or less automatically after a certain period of time had passed since receiving their Bachelor of Arts. In this manner, Tolkien was given his M.A. in October 1919.) But with the student population still depleted, academic postings were nearly impossible to come by. When Tolkien met with William Craigie, his former tutor in Old Icelandic invited him to join the staff of the *Oxford English Dictionary*, also known as the *OED*. In January 1919, once again living in Oxford but this time with a wife and son, Tolkien began work as an assistant lexicographer and was assigned to words beginning with *W*.

During the year and a half that he served on the staff of the *Oxford English Dictionary*, Tolkien wrote definitions, compiled etymologies, and tracked down the earliest recorded uses of a list of words that included *waggle, waistcoat, waiter, wallop, walnut, walrus, wampum, wanderer, warm, wasp, warlock, wild,*

71

winter, and *wold.* He later reported that he learned more in those months working as a lexicographer than during any other equal period of time in his life. It should be noted that long after Tolkien's work at the dictionary was over, two words from his fiction were deemed to have achieved currency in English, and because of this, *hobbit* and *orc* were added to the *OED*.

After getting settled back in Oxford, Tolkien also began to accept students. Because he was married, he was particularly sought out to serve as the tutor for pupils from women's colleges such as St. Hugh's, St. Hilda's, Somerville, and Lady Margaret Hall, since when they came to the Tolkiens' home for lessons, they would not require a chaperone to come with them.

In 1920 Tolkien was offered a post at Leeds University, located about 160 miles north of Oxford, where he would teach for the next five years, beginning first at the rank of Reader, but being appointed to a new Professorship in English Language in 1924 at the rather young age of thirty-two. During his time at Leeds, Tolkien collaborated with E. V. Gordon on a new edition of the Middle English poem *Sir Gawain and the Green Knight,* which would go on to become the most widely used text of the poem studied in Britain and the U.S. Together Tolkien and Gordon also helped to found the Leeds Viking Club, an informal organization dedicated to singing and reading Old Icelandic sagas—as well as to a good deal of beer drinking and merriment as members of the club recited original songs and poems, some serious but many comic, in Old English, Gothic, Old Norse, and other extinct Germanic languages.

Tolkien's professional activity during this time was notable—especially his co-editing of *Sir Gawain and the Green Knight* and also his *Middle English Vocabulary*, published in 1922. This scholarly output, combined with his ability and his willingness to work closely with students—motivating, nurturing, and pushing them—made him a popular and respected faculty member at Leeds. These attributes would soon make him a strong candidate for a more-prestigious position at one of England's most prestigious universities.

At Leeds Tolkien developed a pattern he would display for the rest of his working life. In the midst of all his other duties—tutoring, preparing and giving lectures, grading, conducting scholarly research in his discipline, and attending the never-ending succession of meetings that take place at a university—he would persevere in his cycle of working on his poems and stories, setting them aside for a while, and then revising and rewriting them again and again. Among other fictional works, it was during this time that Tolkien wrote "The Cat and the Fiddle," an early version of the song Frodo sings at The Prancing Pony in chapter 9 of *The Fellowship of the Ring*, and "The Root of the Boot," an early version of the delightful "The Stone Troll" song that Sam sings three chapters later.

In the summer of 1925, a position at Oxford became open. Knowing that his candidacy was somewhat of a long shot, Tolkien carefully crafted a letter dated June 27 to the Electors of the Rawlinson and Bosworth Professorship of Anglo-Saxon, which began: "Gentlemen, I desire to offer myself as a candidate."

Professor Tolkien, as we should now call him, since this was his title at Leeds, then went on to summarize his academic history so far. Careful readers may note that like job-seekers past and present, he did not mention his greatest liability—his poor performance on his Honor Mods. He also chose to mention the year he *accepted* the position at the *OED* rather than the year that he actually started work, perhaps to make his tenure there look longer. Tolkien wrote:

> I entered Exeter College as Stapledon Exhibitioner in 1911. After taking Classical Moderations in 1913 (in which I specialized in Greek philology), I graduated with first class honors in English in 1915, my special subject being Old Icelandic. Until the end of 1918 I held a commission in the Lancashire Fusiliers, and at that date entered the service of the Oxford English Dictionary.... In October 1920 I went to Leeds as Reader in English Language.

For reasons not quite clear, Tolkien also declined to mention that he had been made a Professor at Leeds nine months earlier.

Perhaps he was concerned that seeking a second professorship after holding his first appointment for only nine months might be seen as a lack of commitment. He went on to explain that the large amount of teaching he was required to do at Leeds had kept him from doing as much scholarly work as he would have liked, so it might have confused the issue to mention that for the past academic year, due to his promotion from Reader to Professor, he had, in fact, had been allowed more time for research.

Whatever his reasons for failing to mention his new position at Leeds, Tolkien ended his letter of application by promising that if elected to the Rawlinson and Bosworth Chair at Oxford, he would endeavor to make productive use of the many opportunities it would offer for research, that he would advance to the best of his ability the "growing neighborliness of linguistic and literary studies," and that he would continue to encourage "philological enthusiasm among the young." Here we find, in Tolkien's tactful wording, his assurance that he would do what he could to mend the growing rift between the linguistic and the literary sides of English studies at Oxford, but that at the same time he would promote the linguistic or philological side—actions he knew the selection committee desired from a candidate.

To his great surprise, the thirty-three-year-old Tolkien was offered the prestigious post.

In his letter of resignation to the Leeds Vice Chancellor,

we can hear Tolkien's discomfort at leaving the professor's chair so recently awarded him. In spite of his unexpected turn of good fortune, Tolkien states that he had feelings of "great regret" at the sudden severance of ties. He explains that while the chair at Oxford was a goal he dreamed he might attain in the "more distant years," the sudden resignation of his predecessor made it possible much sooner than he had ever anticipated. Although the Oxford posting was far more esteemed, in Tolkien's closing we find an honest expression of his enjoyment of his time at Leeds, as he confesses to the Vice Chancellor: "After this University's kindness, and the great happiness of my brief period of work here, I feel ungrateful in asking to be released from my appointment so soon."

After a brief period of overlap where he served at both universities, in January 1926 Tolkien moved his family back to Oxford, a family that now included three sons: John, Michael, and the most recent addition, Christopher, named after Christopher Wiseman. Tolkien was now one of the youngest professors at one of the world's oldest and most-esteemed universities.

There would be several moves within Oxford as the family grew larger to include a fourth child—this time, to Edith's delight, a daughter—and then slowly became smaller as, one by one, the children all grew up and left home. And there would be one more promotion, as Tolkien would become Merton Professor of English Language and Literature in 1945. But except for a brief period of three years quite late in life when he and Edith would live in Bournemouth on England's southern coast, Tolkien would remain at Oxford, and Oxford would be his home.

"And after this, you might say, nothing else really happened," Humphrey Carpenter jumps in to state about a third of the way into his roughly three-hundred-page biography. He continues by noting:

> Tolkien came back to Oxford, was Rawlinson and Bosworth Professor of Anglo-Saxon for twenty years, was then elected Merton Professor of English Language and Literature, went to live in a conventional Oxford suburb where he spent the first part of his retirement, moved to a nondescript seaside resort, came back to Oxford after his wife died, and himself died a peaceful death at the age of eighty-one. It was the ordinary unremarkable life led by countless other scholars; a life of academic brilliance, certainly, but only in a very narrow professional field that is really of little interest to laymen.

"And that would be that," Carpenter concludes. "Apart from the strange fact that during these years when 'nothing happened,' he wrote two books which have become world best-sellers."

World best-sellers—when we are talking about *The Hobbit*

and *The Lord of the Rings*, the term almost seems an understatement, for it fails to adequately describe the sensation these two works of literature would cause and the intense devotion readers of all ages from all over the world and all sorts of backgrounds would come to have for them.

COALBITERS, C. S. LEWIS, AND INKLINGS

In his role as Rawlinson and Bosworth Professor of Anglo-Saxon at Oxford, Tolkien was required to give a minimum of thirty-six lectures or classes a year. But in keeping with his promise to encourage philological enthusiasm, and because he deemed this number insufficient to cover the material he felt needed to be covered, Tolkien typically went well beyond the minimum. In his second year alone, Tolkien gave 136 classes or lectures, one hundred more than the terms of his chair demanded.

At Leeds, Tolkien had been considered to be a good teacher by both the students and his colleagues, and he continued to be so at Oxford. Encouraging enthusiasm among his students was easy because Tolkien himself was enthusiastic about the subjects he taught, and had been ever since he was a boy. Tolkien did have a weakness: students at his lectures had to concentrate especially hard due to his rapid and sometimes difficult to understand speech. His strengths continued to be the way he brought ancient texts, such as *Beowulf*, to life. And here his sensitivity to word—as both a philologist and a poet—was put to good use. Tolkien was one of those rare academics who conveyed not only the sound and meaning of the ancient works he specialized in but also their heart and soul. During those times when he recited passages from Old English, his students were transported back to an Anglo-Saxon mead hall, and Tolkien became a bard reciting the sagas of old.

W. H. Auden came to Oxford as a biology student in 1925, the same year Tolkien took up the Chair of Anglo-Saxon, but Auden soon changed to the English School where he developed a strong liking for Old English literature. Later in life he described what it was like to attend a lecture by the then-young Professor Tolkien. "At a certain point," Auden recalled, "he recited, and magnificently, a long passage of *Beowulf*. I was spellbound."

At Leeds, Tolkien had helped to found the Viking Club to promote student interest in the Old Norse Sagas. In 1926, he founded the *Kolbitar* or Coalbiters, a group of Oxford dons who met to read and translate the Icelandic sagas and myths. The name referred to those who huddle so close to the fire on a winter's night that they seem to bite the coals. Initially its members were limited to faculty who had a knowledge of

Icelandic, but soon the informal club was expanded to welcome faculty who were better classified as interested beginners.

One of these interested beginners was a young don from Magdalen College who found the meetings exhilarating. His name was Clive Staples Lewis.

Six years younger than Tolkien, Lewis had been a student at Oxford from 1917 to 1923. Unlike Tolkien, Lewis had aced his Honor Mods and been awarded a rare Triple First on his finals, earning degrees in both philosophy and in English. Lewis, too, had fought in France during World War I. While Tolkien had been sent home with trench fever, shrapnel wounds had brought an end to Lewis's military service six months after he arrived at the front.

Lewis had been made a Fellow of Magdalen College in 1925. So despite their difference in age and Tolkien's previous experience at Leeds, both were relatively new to the Oxford faculty when they met on the afternoon of May 11, 1926, at a meeting of the English School.

Though no one could have guessed it at the time, it was a meeting that would change the course of both of their lives.

Tolkien was a serious Christian and a Catholic. Lewis was an equally serious atheist. What is more, having been born in Belfast, Northern Ireland, Lewis had been exposed firsthand to the "Troubles" between Catholics and Protestants and had been warned all his life about trusting a "Papist," as Catholics were called by Lewis's Ulster Protestant relatives. What Tolkien and Lewis shared in common was a love for myths, especially northern ones. And so not long after their first meeting, Tolkien invited Lewis to join the Coalbiters.

On June 26, 1927, Lewis reported to his friend Arthur Greeves: "We have so far read the *Younger Edda* and the *Volsung Saga*. . . . You will be able to imagine what a delight this is to me, and how, even in turning over the pages of my *Icelandic Dictionary*, the mere name of god or giant catching my eye will sometimes throw me . . . into a wild dream of northern skies and Valkyrie music."

Of the first few years of Lewis and Tolkien's growing friendship, there is relatively little recorded. On December 3, 1929, Lewis wrote to Arthur, saying that he had gotten himself into a whirl as he always did at the end of the term. At this point he had just turned thirty-one and had been an Oxford don for four years. He then described for Arthur something wonderful that had happened that week: "I was up till 2:30 on Monday, talking to the AngloSaxon professor Tolkien who came with me to College from a society and sat discoursing of the gods and giants and Asgard for three hours, then departing in the wind and rain." Lewis concluded: "The fire was bright and the talk good."

Lewis's invitation to Tolkien that he come back to his rooms at Magdalen for some good talk—just the two of them—ushered in the next step in their friendship. During their discussion, which lasted into the early-morning hours, Tolkien came to see that Lewis was one of those rare people in the world who might just like the strange *Lost Tales* he had been writing and rewriting off and on since coming home from the war in 1917.

A few days after their late-night conversation about the Norse gods and giants, Tolkien loaned Lewis "The Gest of Beren and Luthien." It was quite long, still unfinished, and written in rhyming couplets. Doubting that anyone besides himself would have any interest in this kind of story, before giving it to Lewis, Tolkien had shown it to almost no one.

What would Lewis think of it? Would he think it worth reading and commenting on, or would he find it antiquated, eccentric, or simply bizarre?

A few days later, on December 7, 1929, Lewis wrote to Tolkien: "Just a line to say that I sat up late last night and have read the *gest* as far as to where Beren and his gnomish allies defeat the patrol of the orcs. . . . I can honestly say that it is ages since I have had an evening of such delight." Besides the mythical value in the piece, which he praised, Lewis also reported that he found a deep *sense of reality* in the poem's background, a trait that would characterize all of Tolkien's epic fantasy.

After years of writing stories Tolkien thought might never be made public, in Lewis he had found a highly appreciative and approving audience. In the weeks that followed, he began to share more of his work. And Lewis responded to Tolkien's initiative by sharing some poems of his own.

In a letter written some months later to his brother, Lewis offered a description of what an ordinary day for him at Oxford was like and pointed out that on Mondays, since he did not have any pupils, he used the time to correct papers. "It has also become a regular custom that Tolkien should drop in on me of a Monday morning and drink a glass," Lewis wrote. Sometimes in addition to critiquing each other's writing they would talk English School politics, theology, or the general state of the nation. Lewis confessed that these regular meetings with Tolkien were "one of the pleasantest spots in the week."

And so began one of the world's greatest literary friendships.

Decades later Tolkien would write of the "unpayable debt" he owed for the "sheer encouragement" Lewis had offered him over the years. "He was for long my only audience," Tolkien explained. "Only from him did I ever get the idea that my 'stuff' could be more than a private hobby."

He was for long my only audience. Before the Inklings were formed, before the world was given *The Hobbit,* and long before millions and millions of readers all over the world would come to love *The Lord of the Rings*—Tolkien met with just Lewis to read aloud his stuff from *The Book of Lost Tales.*

It is safe to say that without Lewis's encouragement, there would have been no *Lord of the Rings,* for when Tolkien got discouraged and stopped altogether, Lewis would always be there, insisting on more. Likewise, it would be through Tolkien's assistance, and many in-depth discussions and debates on the subject, that Lewis the serious atheist would come to a belief in Christ. And without Tolkien's Christian influence, there would have been no *Screwtape Letters*, no *Mere Christianity*, and no Narnia.

"Friendship with Lewis compensates for much," Tolkien would later write in his diary. In the years to come, he would face the strain of bringing up four children on an academic's modest salary and the frustration of never having enough time to be both a serious writer and a serious Oxford scholar.

Friendship with Lewis compensates for much. There would be further strains on Tolkien as over time Edith began to resent his Catholicism and the fact that she had been made to convert. Tolkien noted that Lewis was "honest, brave, intellectual—a scholar, a poet, and a philosopher—and a lover...after a long pilgrimage, of Our Lord," and he concluded that friendship with Lewis gave him a great deal of pleasure and comfort. But more than this, Tolkien saw that Lewis's friendship had also done him "much good."

During his first years after arriving back at Oxford as a professor in 1925, Tolkien was meeting regularly with the Coalbiters to read Icelandic more or less publicly, and with Lewis to read their own works in private. What was missing was a broader forum where their own writing could be read aloud, critiqued, and revised. Lewis and Tolkien seemed to recognize this need, for they began to attend a writers club of a type common in those days. This writers group had been founded by an Oxford student—though he also had invited some faculty to join. Like many student groups, it was not long-lived. After it died out, it was reinvented as a group of Lewis's friends who met in his rooms at Magdalen on Thursday evenings (where the emphasis was on reading their works-in-progress) and in a favorite pub, often The Eagle and Child, on Tuesday mornings (where the emphasis was on good conversation). This second incarnation of the Inklings—for this was the name of both groups—lasted much longer than the first and met regularly for seventeen years from 1933 to 1949, and met irregularly for many years afterward.

When Tolkien was in his mid-seventies and beginning to witness his works acquire worldwide fame, he received a question about how the Inklings began and where the name came from. In a letter dated September 11, 1967, he wrote the following response:

> The name was not invented by C. S. Lewis (nor by me). In origin it was an undergraduate jest, devised as the name of a literary (or writers') club. The founder was an undergraduate at University College, named Tangye Lean.... Both

C.S.L. and I became members. The club met
in T.L.'s room in University College: its pro-
cedure was that at each meeting members
should read aloud, unpublished compositions.
These were supposed to be open to immediate
criticism. . . . The club soon died. . . . Its name
was then transferred (by C.S.L.) to the unde-
termined and unelected circle of friends who
gathered about C.S.L., and met in his rooms in
Magdalen.

This circle that gathered around Lewis was, in one sense,
a rather conservative group of thinkers who held traditional,
we could even say orthodox, views about literature, the Christian faith, and life in general. In this way they stood in stark
contrast to their contemporaries at Oxford who believed that
any notion of truth or beauty in literature was a subjective con-
struct and life itself was merely a result of random chance with
no purpose or plan other than what one chose to give it. In another sense, the Inklings were both radical and revolutionary.
The English writer John Wain, himself an occasional Inkling
in the 1940s, saw the groups as "a circle of instigators, almost
of incendiaries, meeting to urge one another on in the task of
redirecting the whole current of contemporary art and life."

A typical meeting would consist of around six or seven
members. Nearly always present were Lewis—known to

his friends as Jack—his brother Warren, Lewis's very literary physician Dr. "Humphrey" Havard, and Tolkien. Hugo
Dyson and Owen Barfield also attended, though less regularly.
Charles Williams would join the group six or seven years after
its creation when the bombing during World War II forced the
London offices of Oxford University Press, where Williams
worked as an editor, to relocate.

When the war broke out, Warren Lewis ("Warnie") was
called back into service and stationed in Yorkshire. Through
regular correspondence, some of it quite lengthy, Lewis en-
deavored to keep his brother informed about local events and
distracted from global ones. In a letter to Warnie written in
November 1939, Lewis reported:

> On Thursday we had a meeting of the Ink-
> lings. . . . I have never in my life seen Dyson so
> exuberant—"a roaring cataract of nonsense."
> The bill of fare afterwards consisted of a section
> of the new Hobbit book from Tolkien, a nativity
> play from Williams (unusually intelligible for
> him, and approved by all), and a chapter out of
> the book on the Problem of Pain from me.

The new Hobbit book that Lewis mentions here was an
early draft of what would become *The Lord of the Rings*. The
"unusually intelligible" nativity play by Charles Williams was
The House by the Stable. Lewis noted that along with his own

chapter, the three readings that night almost seemed to fit together in a logical sequence. Borrowing a phrase from Pope's *Essay on Man*, he wished that Warnie could have been there to enjoy a "first-rate evening's talk of the usual wide-ranging kind" with works that went "from grave to gay, from lively to severe."

Years afterward Warnie would include his own account of a typical Inklings meeting in his essay "Memoir of C. S. Lewis." There Warnie recalled:

> There were no rules, officers, agendas or formal
> elections—unless one counts it as a rule that we
> met in Jack's rooms at Magdalen every Thurs-
> day evening after dinner....When half a dozen
> or so had arrived, tea would be produced, and
> then when pipes were well alight Jack would say,
> "Well, has nobody got anything to read us?"
> Out would come a manuscript, and we would
> settle down to sit in judgment upon it—real un-
> biased judgment, too, since we were no mutual
> admiration society.

Out of the hammer-and-tongs critique offered by the group—razor-sharp criticism when necessary and bounteous praise when merited—would come some of the most amazing stories the world had ever seen, among them *The Hobbit* and *The Lord of the Rings*.

MR. BILBO BAGGINS OF BAG END

On a warm summer's day in 1930, John Ronald Reuel Tolkien gazed out his study window at Number 20 Northmoor Road to the garden in the backyard and then to the green, suburban countryside beyond. Then he looked at the tall stack of School Certificate Exams he had been sent to mark and let out a deep sigh.

There would be no time to work in the garden or go for a walk, not today.

While today the salary of university professors can reach six figures, particularly at major research institutions, this has not always been the case. Back in 1930, the middle-aged Oxford professor and father of four—the youngest, Priscilla, having been added to the family the year before—barely made enough to support his family in the style in which Oxford professors (however underpaid) were expected to do. Besides all the normal expenses, there were now the boys' tuition costs at private school to worry about, as well as a new mortgage after the family's move from the smaller Number 22 next door.

So while his colleagues who had more inherited wealth or fewer children were enjoying a holiday at the seashore or simply relaxing in the ease of summer vacation, to earn extra money Professor Tolkien took on what for him were dull and tedious grading duties.

The School Certificate, the predecessor of today's O-Level Exams, was an optional test taken by British high school students around the time they turned sixteen. Those hoping to receive a Certificate were tested in mathematics, English, and three other subjects. Professor Tolkien's task was to read and mark the English section of each and every test as either: Failure, Pass, Credit (a higher pass), or Distinction (the highest pass).

In an interview with the BBC years later, Tolkien described what happened next:

> I can still see the corner of my house in 20 Northmoor Road where it happened. I had an enormous pile of exam papers there. Marking school examinations in the summertime is very laborious and unfortunately also *boring*. And I remember picking up a paper and actually finding—I nearly gave an extra mark for it; an extra five marks actually—there was one page of this particular paper that was left blank. Glorious! Nothing to read. So I scribbled on it, I can't think why: *In a hole in the ground there lived a hobbit.*

We are left to wonder. Had Professor Tolkien not desperately needed the money that grading the exams provided, had there not been so many of them (Tolkien later explained that he had more than two hundred to grade), had the task not been so tedious, and had there not been a blank page left in one exam booklet, is it possible there might never have been the story we know today as *The Hobbit*?

Perhaps.

In a hole in the ground there lived a hobbit.

So what was a hobbit? Tolkien had no idea. "Names always generate a story in my mind," he later noted. "Eventually I thought I'd better find out what hobbits were like."

Tolkien often had made up stories to entertain his children in the evening. Sometimes they were just told as he made them up, sometimes he wrote them out first and then read them. There had been the story of Carrots, a boy with red hair who climbed inside a cuckoo clock and went on a series of strange adventures. One time after Michael lost a beloved toy dog on the beach, his father had created "Roverandom," a story about a young dog named Rover who is turned into a toy by a bad-tempered wizard. There was another story drawn from a Dutch doll that belonged to Michael, named Tom Bombadil— who would later become a character in *The Lord of the Rings*. And there were also the annual *Letters from Father Christmas,* which Tolkien wrote, illustrated, and then had delivered to the house each December.

The earliest version of *The Hobbit* was begun by Tolkien in 1930 merely as another of the many stories created for

John, Micheal, and Christopher—Priscilla being too young at the time. Gradually, the boys began to notice discrepancies in its retelling, so Tolkien began to write down what previously had been an oral story. In the foreword to the 50th Anniversary Edition of *The Hobbit*, published in 1987, we find Michael's memories of sitting with his two brothers on their father's study floor as chapters from this new story were read to them, and of Christopher, who was around five at the time, interrupting their father with concerns about the details—on one occasion blurting out: "Last time, you said Bilbo's front door was blue, and you said Thorin had a golden tassel on his hood, but you've just said that Bilbo's front door was green, and the tassel on Thorin's hood was silver."

"Damn the boy!" his father had muttered and then went over to his desk and made a note of the correction.

For a long time, the story of Bilbo Baggins was not known to anyone beside Tolkien's children and C. S. Lewis, who had shown an interest in the bedtime story and had been loaned the typed copy.

"Since term began I have had a delightful time reading a children's story which Tolkien has just written," Lewis wrote to Arthur Greeves on February 4, 1933. "It is so exactly like what we would both have longed to write." Lewis went on to point out that while reading the story, he felt that rather than making something up, Tolkien seemed to be describing a world that he had somehow been able to enter.

And so four people in the world, the Tolkien boys and C. S. Lewis, had read or had been read *The Hobbit*. And it very nearly ended there. Despite the fact that it was put down on paper, Tolkien's story about Mr. Bilbo Baggins of Bag End nearly suffered the fate of so many others like it that Tolkien had told his children before and nearly remained just a bedtime story, and an unfinished one at that.

How did *The Hobbit* come to be more than just something written to entertain Tolkien's children? In a letter dated July 16, 1964, looking back on the remarkable story of how *The Hobbit* came to be published, Tolkien pointed out, "*The Hobbit* saw the light and made my connection with Allen & Unwin by accident."

The Hobbit came to be published *by accident*? Later Tolkien would have Gandalf suggest to Frodo that what at the time may seem to be mere chance, looking back later may be seen as the workings of something far greater.

It just so happened that a friend of the Tolkien family, the Reverend Mother St. Teresa Gale, who was the Mother Superior at Cherwell Edge, a nearby convent, came down with the flu. And so, as Tolkien explained, in order to "amuse her while recovering," he loaned her the typed manuscript—a manuscript which, it should be pointed out, was not quite finished and ended with the death of Smaug. "Whether it amused her or not, I never heard," Tolkien noted.

And once again, it very nearly ended there.

But it just so happened that one of Tolkien's former students, Elaine Griffiths, was tutoring undergraduates at Cherwell Edge at the time and was a resident in the hostel there. She heard about the odd but amazing story written by her former tutor, which had been loaned to the Mother Superior, and received permission from Tolkien to borrow the manuscript next. Elaine Griffiths read the story and liked it. After finishing it, Griffiths returned the manuscript to her professor.

And once more, it very nearly ended there.

But it just so happened that Elaine Griffiths was friends with a former Oxford student named Susan Dagnall, who also had studied English with Professor Tolkien. After graduating, Dagnall had gone to London to work for a publishing firm. One of her projects was to supervise a revision of the modern English translation of *Beowulf*. Tolkien had been asked to direct this revision but was unable to fit it into his schedule. He had recommended that Elaine Griffiths be assigned the task. Sometime in early 1936, Dagnall came to Oxford to discuss the project with Griffiths. While Dagnall was there, as later explained in an interview, Elaine Griffiths offered her friend an unrelated piece of advice: "I'll tell you something, go along to Professor Tolkien and see if you can get out of him a work called *The Hobbit*. I think it's frightfully good."

Susan Dagnall borrowed the manuscript from her former

professor and brought it back with her to the publishing firm she worked at in London, which just so happened to be Allen & Unwin. Dagnall also thought the story frightfully good, and urged Tolkien to finish it as soon as possible and submit it formally to Allen & Unwin for consideration.

I think it's frightfully good. At this point it is worth pausing to ask: Why had Elaine Griffiths (an Oxford graduate who had majored in English and studied the finest works of literature ever written), why had C. S. Lewis (not only a scholar but a writer himself with extremely high standards), and why had Susan Dagnall (an editor at a publishing house that had an endless supply of *finished* manuscripts to consider) all been so favorably impressed by a story Tolkien had initially written to entertain his children? What was it about *The Hobbit* that made it so remarkable and so different from Tolkien's previous bedtime stories?

We can find a partial answer in a letter Tolkien wrote to Christopher Bretherton in 1964, long after *The Hobbit* and *The Lord of the Rings* were published. Tolkien pointed out that while his children were young, he had invented many stories for them. "None of these have been published," Tolkien noted. And in these six words he makes it clear that there was something which gave *The Hobbit* a broader appeal and set it apart from the others.

Tolkien noted that at the time he was writing *The Hobbit*,

he already had put his materials about the "Elder Days" into a coherent form. He had not—and would never completely—finished *The Book of Lost Tales*, but there was a cohesion, all the major details were there. While *The Hobbit* originally was intended to be just another of Tolkien's lighthearted stories for children, Tolkien told Bretherton that gradually it became mixed together with his mythology, and it was this that gave *The Hobbit* its "impression of historical depth" and caused it to become both larger and more heroic than his other stories.

In a different letter, Tolkien would describe the connection between *The Hobbit* and his legends of an earlier time by stating: "I did not know as I began it that it belonged."

Though Tolkien would submit the collection of stories from *The Book of Lost Tales* for publication a number of times, the book we know today as *The Silmarillion* would not be published until 1977, four years after his death, when his worldwide fan base was hungry for anything more he had written. While these stories from the dawn of Middle-earth would never have anything near the appeal of Tolkien's two great masterpieces, without them he never could have written *The Hobbit* or *The Lord of the Rings*.

Biographer Humphrey Carpenter describes the previously separate parts of Tolkien's creativity that came together in *The Hobbit* this way:

Tolkien's imagination was running along two distinct courses that did not meet. On one side were the stories composed for mere amusement...for the entertainment of his children. On the other were the grander themes...associated with his own legends. Meanwhile nothing was reaching print, beyond a few poems in the *Oxford Magazine* which indicated to his colleagues that Tolkien was amused by dragons' hoards and funny little men with names like Tom Bombadil: a harmless pastime....Something was lacking, something that would bind the two sides of his imagination together and produce a story that was at once heroic and mythical and at the same time tuned to the popular imagination.

I did not know as I began it that it belonged.

On that warm summer's day in 1930, when John Ronald Reuel Tolkien scrawled "In a hole in the ground, there lived a hobbit" on that empty page he had come to in an exam booklet, he had no idea he had written the first line of what would become the missing piece in his fiction, the story that would bridge the mythical and the popular. The story that would be both.

After Susan Dagnall's request, Tolkien completed the story that followed the death of Smaug in what for him was record time. Among the new chapters were "Not at Home," "The Clouds Burst," "The Return Journey," and "The Last

Stage." On October 3, 1936, Tolkien finished retyping the entire manuscript and mailed off a copy with the new chapters to Allen & Unwin. Four weeks later, ten-year-old Rayner Unwin wrote his now famous review (discussed earlier in the prologue) and received his shilling.

On December 2, 1936, Stanley Unwin officially accepted *The Hobbit* for publication, and the wheels of the production department at Allen & Unwin were set in motion. There then followed many discussions back and forth about the text, the maps, and the illustrations—the latter two which Tolkien drew himself (adding to the cost of making the book, but a huge success with readers, despite the fact that in his review, Rayner Unwin had suggested no illustrations would be necessary). In 1937 alone Tolkien wrote twenty-six letters to Allen & Unwin and received thirty-one. After numerous revisions Tolkien made to the proofs, some quite extensive—a trait that would be typical of him, giving the typesetting team fits—*The Hobbit* was published on September 21, 1937.

"Oxford is mildly aroused," Tolkien wrote to Stanley Unwin three weeks later. "My own college is I think good for six copies." Despite Tolkien's underwhelming report of interest and sales, the first print run of 1,500 copies quickly sold out, and a second printing was rushed through to be ready in time for Christmas. Hobbit-mania—though starting off relatively calmly—would over the coming years, slowly but steadily, become anything but calm.

The "New Hobbit"

On October 2, 1937, eleven days after its release, the first review of *The Hobbit* appeared. The reviewer in the *Times Literary Supplement*—C. S. Lewis writing anonymously —declared that *The Hobbit* belonged to that very small class of books that admits us to a world of its own, one that somehow "seems to have been going on before we stumbled into it." To define the world found in *The Hobbit*, Lewis maintained, was impossible because it is a world we cannot anticipate before we go there—but having once visited, it is one we can never forget. To call *The Hobbit* a children's book, Lewis pointed out, was true only in the sense that the first of many readings could be undertaken while readers are young. "Prediction is dangerous," he concluded, "but *The Hobbit* may well prove a classic."

On October 11, 1937—barely three weeks after *The Hobbit* was released—Stanley Unwin wrote to Tolkien, confident of sales and expressing interest in a second book. "*The Hobbit* has come to stay," Unwin told him. "A large public will be clamoring next year to hear more from you about Hobbits."

Like all publishers, Stanley Unwin wanted a sequel that

met two essential criteria: the second book had to be much like the first, and it had to be finished quickly, ideally in time for Christmas. What Stanley Unwin eventually got from Tolkien would be nothing like what he had requested.

It would be far better.

"I am a little perturbed," Tolkien wrote back several days later, on October 15, 1937. "I cannot think of anything more to say about hobbits." But he promised that if, in fact, there was reader interest for a sequel, he would try to come up with something in a style that was similar. In the meantime, Tolkien wondered, might Allen & Unwin be willing to look at some of his other works which, for the most part, were already finished?

On November 15, 1937, Tolkien went to London for a lunch where he and Stanley Unwin met in person for the first time. Afterward, Tolkien submitted for consideration a collection of myths he called *The Silmarillion* and an assortment of children's stories—among them "Mr. Bliss," "Farmer Giles of Ham," and "Roverandom," as well as his series of *Letters from Father Christmas*.

Through a prolonged series of letters back and forth, Tolkien was gently but firmly informed that none of these materials he had submitted were deemed suitable for publication. What Allen & Unwin wanted was another book like *The Hobbit*. Could he please try to write one and do so as quickly as possible? But try as he might, Tolkien could not write another book like *The Hobbit*. The only story he could write that included hobbits was something much darker, far longer, and a great deal more complicated.

The letters exchanged between Tolkien and his publisher in the ensuing years would revisit these same issues again and again. From Allen & Unwin came repeated expressions of interest in another book like *The Hobbit*. From Tolkien came repeated expressions of concern that his "New Hobbit" was not turning out to be much like a sequel as it continued to expand in size and scope and with each successive chapter was not even close to being finished. And in the interim, were the editors at Allen & Unwin still sure they did not want to publish *The Silmarillion* or one of his children's stories?

An early version of the new story began again with Bilbo Baggins. At this point the hobbit has run out of the money he returned with at the end of the first tale. At a party he gives to celebrate his birthday, he slips on his magic ring and sets off in search of more dragon gold. Tolkien soon revised this opening, adding a new character, Bilbo's son, to be the hero of this second story. This character, originally named Bingo Bolger-Baggins, was soon changed to be Bilbo's nephew. What exactly Bingo would do was a problem, but perhaps it might have something to do with the ring Bilbo had found.

On February 1, 1938, Tolkien wrote to ask if Rayner Unwin, now age twelve, might be willing to read a first chapter, which he had entitled "A Long-expected Party." Two weeks later Tolkien reported to C. A. Furth, the editor at Allen & Unwin assigned to the project, that he was not able to get beyond this first chapter because he had used up all his ideas about hobbits in writing the first book. Near the start of March, in a sign of things to come, Tolkien wrote to Stanley Unwin that the sequel now had three chapters but had taken an unpremeditated turn and was getting out of hand.

In July 1938, Tolkien reported that the promised sequel to *The Hobbit* was stopped and confessed that he had no idea what to do with it. By August, Tolkien announced that he had finished nearly seven chapters and that his new story now had a name: *The Lord of the Ring.* That was the good news. The bad news was that the story seemed to have developed a will of its own and was moving in directions that were quite unforeseen. In October, Tolkien wrote to say that he had finished chapter 11, and in one of the greatest underestimations in literary history, stated: "I still live in hopes that I may be able to submit it early next year."

Four months later, on February 2, 1939, Tolkien wrote C. A. Furth that *The Lord of the Rings* had reached chapter 12, was more than three hundred pages long, and was still far from being done. In another great underestimation, Tolkien predicted that it would take him around two hundred pages more to finish. Furth wrote back the next week telling Tolkien that if the new story was going to be published by Christmas, Allen & Unwin would need it by the middle of June at the latest.

Tolkien wrote Furth on February 10, 1939, promising that he would make a special effort to "finish it off" before June 15.

Ten years and nine months later—in October 1949, the exact date is uncertain—after innumerable delays caused by his growing duties at Oxford, family matters, not one but a series of illnesses and injuries, a second world war, and periods of running out of either energy, ideas, or both, Tolkien finally finished *The Lord of the Rings*. Though again, there would be a great many changes and revisions, he now had what is called a fair copy complete and ready to loan to the one person in the world who had been most instrumental in helping him bring it to completion.

C. S. Lewis had heard each chapter read aloud at Inklings meetings, and over the past twelve years he had offered Tolkien numerous suggestions—much of which, according to Lewis, Tolkien simply ignored—and endless encouragement. Now he would be the very first person besides the author himself to read the revised work from start to finish in its entirety.

What would his reaction be?

"I have drained the rich cup and satisfied a long thirst," Lewis wrote Tolkien on October 27, 1949. "*Uton herian holbytlas.*"

Let us praise hobbits! In the years to come, there would be millions of readers who would declare *The Lord of the Rings* to be one of the greatest books of fiction ever written, but Lewis was the first. "Once it really gets under way," Lewis declared, "the steady upward slope of grandeur and terror...is almost unequalled in the whole range of narrative art known to me."

Lewis congratulated his friend on his long-awaited accomplishment. Looking back on all the difficulties Tolkien had encountered since first starting his "New Hobbit" in 1937, all the sorrows and frustrations Tolkien had weathered and all the obstacles he had overcome, Lewis could still say: "All the long years you have spent on it are justified."

In the foreword that he wrote for the second edition of *The Lord of the Rings*, Tolkien sketches out some of the delays he had faced. "Those who had asked for more information about hobbits eventually got it," he begins, "but they had to wait a long time."

Tolkien then describes how he was able to work on his story only after his many other personal and academic duties had been seen to. Using words suggesting that rather than the author of the story, he had been more like a character traveling along with the hobbits, he reports: "I plodded on, mostly by night, till I stood by Balin's tomb in Moria. There I halted for a long while. It was almost a year later when I went on and so came to Lothlorien and the Great River late in 1941."

And this delay of almost an entire year was only one of a number of major delays in the writing.

In addition to the duties normally associated with his academic position, Tolkien confesses to readers in his foreword, "Many other interests as a learner and teacher . . . often absorbed me." One of these other interests that absorbed Tolkien was fairy tales—not merely writing them, but understanding them and their fundamental place in human history. On a cold and windy day in March 1939, Tolkien had boarded a train for the University of St. Andrews in Scotland, where he had been invited to give the prestigious Andrew Lang Lecture. Rather than focusing on a topic directly related to his role as a Professor of Anglo-Saxon, Tolkien had written a lecture entitled "On Fairy-Stories."

In his now-famous lecture, Tolkien set out to demonstrate that rather than being frivolous and suited only for children, fairy tales were, and always had been, worthy of serious attention. In creating a fairy or secondary world, the author—having been, in Tolkien's view, created in the image of God—was assuming the important role of "sub-creator." Rather than being an escape from reality, this special kind of story provided freedom from a narrow and distorted view of existence. Through fairy-stories, Tolkien maintained, we can recover a proper wonder for the real world. By putting ideas he had long held into a written form as he was preparing the lecture,

Tolkien found justification and encouragement for the long process still to come in writing *The Lord of the Rings.*

All the long years you have spent on it are justified.

Even when his many academic duties and other interests had allowed him time to write, much of the delay in finishing his epic had been self-imposed by Tolkien's own perfectionism—a trait that made the creation of *The Lord of the Rings* painstakingly slow, as every chapter was completely rewritten at least twice, and at the same time also made it a masterpiece. In early 1967, Charlotte and Denis Plimmer sent Tolkien the draft of an article they had written for the *Daily Telegraph* following an interview with him. Tolkien wrote back with corrections, noting that among the characteristics they had not mentioned was the fact that he was a "pedant devoted to accuracy, even in what may appear to others unimportant matters." In a letter written to Milton Waldman at Collins, Tolkien pointed out that every part of the long story had been revised many times and noted, "Hardly a word in its 600,000 or more has been unconsidered."

The obituary that appeared in the *Times* following Tolkien's death—which many believe was written by C. S. Lewis years earlier—addressed Tolkien's perfectionism this way: "His standard of self-criticism was high and the mere suggestion of publication usually set him upon a revision, in the course of which so many new ideas occurred to him that where his friends had hoped for the final text of an old work they actually got the first draft of a new one."

All the long years you have spent on it are justified.

Other delays had been due to the fact that Tolkien had not planned out in advance where the story was going. In a case of colossal understatement, he tells readers in the foreword, "This tale grew in the telling."

For example, Tolkien later explained, he was as surprised as his protagonists when Gandalf failed to appear at Bag End on September 22 as promised. So then he had to figure out why and how Gandalf was delayed. Several chapters later when the hobbits arrive at the Prancing Pony in Bree, Frodo notices a mysterious-looking, weather-beaten man sitting in the shadows with a hood hiding most of his face. "Strider sitting in the corner at the inn was a shock," Tolkien wrote to W. H. Auden, "I had no more idea who he was than had Frodo." And so he then had to figure out who this enigmatic figure was.

A different source of delay came from the fact that after Tolkien realized the link that could connect *The Hobbit* to *The Lord of the Rings* was the ring Bilbo had found, he had to go back and retrofit the details in *The Hobbit* to match the story that takes place afterward. In chapter 5, "Riddles in the Dark," as it was first published in 1937, Gollum was less menacing than in the version readers find today, and willing to be bound by the rules of the riddle-game. The prize Bilbo was to have won in their contest was not being shown the way out but the ring itself, which at the time was simply a magic ring that could make its wearer invisible—not Sauron's One Ring. In the original version, Gollum loses the game, and then apologizes for not being able to find the ring (which Bilbo had already picked up). To make amends for not having the present he had promised, Gollum shows the hobbit the way out of the caverns, and the two part ways amicably.

It took Tolkien twelve long years, from 1937 to 1949, to bring *The Lord of the Rings* to completion. It would take another five years before it would be published.

Why the five-year delay between finishing in 1949 and publishing in 1954?

One reason had to do with Tolkien's continued desire to see *The Silmarillion* published. Was there, he wondered, any way that he could leverage Allen & Unwin's desire to publish *The Lord of the Rings* into having both works released?

From the start Allen & Unwin were concerned that *The Silmarillion* was too esoteric, a claim that even some Tolkien fans agreed with when the book finally came out posthumously in 1977. Edited and revised by Christopher Tolkien, the first chapter begins this way:

> It is told among the wise that the First War
> began before Arda was full-shaped, and ere yet
> there was anything that grew or walked upon

earth; and for long Melkor had the upper hand.
But in the midst of the war a spirit of great
strength and hardihood came to the aid of the
Valar, hearing in the far heaven that there was
battle in the Little Kingdom; and Arda was
filled with the sound of his laughter. So came
Tulkas the Strong, whose anger passes like a
mighty wind, scattering cloud and darkness
before it; and Melkor fled before his wrath and
his laughter, and forsook Arda, and there was
peace for a long age.

Allen & Unwin saw little resemblance between *The Hobbit* and this material, and so had little reason to believe that readers who had liked the former would also like and want to purchase the latter.

After Allen & Unwin once again made it clear they were *not* interested in *The Silmarillion*, Tolkien turned instead to Collins, who for over two years—until the production costs and risk factors became evident—seemed to be interested in publishing both lengthy works. Finally after much negotiation and a clear *no* from Collins, in a letter dated June 22, 1952, Tolkien wrote again to Rayner Unwin—who was now twenty-six.

Tolkien himself was now sixty, and, as he explained, years were becoming precious to him. Even though, as he felt the need to repeat once more, he still saw the two works as part of one whole, he had "rather modified" his views—better something than nothing—and was ready, if necessary, to consider publishing just *The Lord of the Rings* without any commitment from Allen & Unwin to also bring out *The Silmarillion.*

Could anything be done, Tolkien asked, to unlock the gates that he himself had previously slammed shut?

Eight days later Rayner Unwin wrote back stating that Allen & Unwin was still interested in publishing *The Lord of the Rings—if the ways and means could be surmounted,* and asked if Tolkien might send him a copy of the typescript by registered mail. Tolkien replied that there was no spare copy, only the one he had typed himself. So on September 19, 1952, Rayner came to Oxford, and the one-and-only finished copy of *The Lord of the Rings* was safely passed from Tolkien's hands into his.

In his memoir, *George Allen & Unwin: A Remembrancer,* Rayner Unwin describes what happened next in what had become an epic story of bringing *The Lord of the Rings*—a lengthy and expensive book, full of special characters and maps—to publication:

> My calculations indicated that we stood to lose
> £1000 if we published it with moderate suc-
> cess.... In the autumn of 1952, I was just a year
> old in publishing, and working strictly outside

my job-description in dealing with authors at
all.... I took my figures and my problem to
those who had been left in charge during father's
absence.... They suggested I get the go-ahead
from father. He was in Tokyo at the time, so I
wrote an air-letter outlining the quandary.

In a now-famous cable Stanley Unwin wrote back: "*If* you
believe it is a work of genius, *then* you may lose a thousand
pounds."

Once again, Rayner Unwin held the future of Middle-
earth in his hands. And once again, *The Lord of the Rings* was
nearly a book that wasn't. But believing that *The Lord of the
Rings* was indeed a work of genius, the kind of book that would
be worth losing £1,000 of Allen & Unwin's money on, he
decided to risk it. On November 10, 1952, Tolkien received
official notice that Allen & Unwin was ready and willing to
bring the long-awaited sequel to *The Hobbit* to publication.

Tolkien immediately wrote to C. S. Lewis, his supporter
over the long years, with the good news. In a letter dated November 13, 1952, Lewis wrote back with congratulations. "So
much of your whole life, so much of our joint life," Lewis commented, "seemed to be slipping away ... into the past" without
any trace. But now, with *The Lord of the Rings* to come out
in print, there would be a lasting marker of all they had gone
through together in its creation. Lewis noted the toll that all

the years' work had taken on his friend, but promised Tolkien: "There'll be a new ripeness and freedom when the book's out."

Besides the long wait due to Tolkien's desire for a contract that would include both *The Lord of the Rings* and *The Silmarillion*, a second reason for the delay had to do with Tolkien's continued perfectionism. Time after time when Tolkien promised Allen & Unwin he would be finished with *The Lord of the Rings* and ready to go to print, he wasn't.

The contract Tolkien received from Allen & Unwin stipulated a manuscript delivery date of March 25, 1953. At that point he was to have a fully completed text to send the printers. On March 24, he wrote Rayner Unwin asking for "lenience in the matter of the date." On April 11, Tolkien wrote again, promising he would have *the first volume* in the mail on the following Monday. Further delays occurred when overzealous copy editors took it upon themselves to correct the Oxford professor's spelling. Without consulting with the author, every occurrence of *dwarves* was changed to *dwarfs*, *elvish* to *elfish*, and *elven* to *elfin*. After Tolkien discovered what had been done, every *dwarfs*, *elfish*, and *elfin* had to be changed back.

A third reason for the delay in publication had to do with the exceptional length of *The Lord of the Rings* and the unusually high price of paper in England in the decade following World War II. A cost analysis done by Rayner Unwin revealed that publishing the work in one big volume—as Tolkien intended it—would make a book that was beyond the means of many readers and lending libraries. The only way to make *The Lord of the Rings* affordable was to break it into a trilogy. A debate over whether to break up the book at all, and then over what to call the three books we know today as *The Fellowship of the Ring*, *The Two Towers*, and *The Return of the King*, added a further delay. As late as January 1954, Tolkien was still negotiating about the titles and complained—unsuccessfully, as it turned out—to Rayner Unwin that he was "not at all happy" about the title *The Two Towers*. In addition, Tolkien preferred *The War of the Ring* as the title of the third book since, in his opinion, *The Return of the King* gave away the all-important ending.

Despite all the obstacles in bringing *The Lord of the Rings* to production, eventually, one by one, they were surmounted, and each volume in turn was sent on to be printed.

An earlier letter from Tolkien to Stanley Unwin summed up his feelings after completing his long epic. "It is written in my life-blood," Tolkien declared, "such as that is, thick or thin; and I can no other."

EPILOGUE

"I am dreading the publication, for it will be impossible not to mind what is said," Tolkien wrote to a friend in December 1953. "I have exposed my heart to be shot at." Seven months later, on July 29, 1954, despite all the holdups and all the setbacks, *The Fellowship of the Ring* was released. It had been nearly seventeen years since *The Hobbit* had been published. Tolkien began working on the so-called sequel when he was forty-five. He was now sixty-two.

The Lord of the Rings, or at least its first volume, was finally published.

In the foreword to the first edition, Tolkien acknowledged the importance of fans of *The Hobbit* who had never stopped hoping for a second story, his four children who had assisted in a variety of ways, and the writing group who over the years had heard many different versions of the tale.

"I dedicate this book to all admirers of Bilbo, but especially to my sons and daughter, and to my friends the Inklings," Tolkien wrote. "To the Inklings, because they have already listened to it with a patience, and indeed with an interest, that almost leads me to suspect that they have hobbit-blood in their venerable ancestry. To my sons and my daughter for the same reason, and also because they have all helped me in the labors of composition."

The Two Towers came out four months later, on November 11, 1954. And after a longer interval than intended, due to the fact that Tolkien still had not finished the promised appendices, *The Return of the King* was released on October 20, 1955.

The fact that the release of the third volume had to be delayed was especially distressing to readers who had just finished *The Two Towers*. In the final chapter Sam realizes that Frodo had not been killed by Shelob's venomous sting, as it had appeared, he only had been drugged. In the book's very last paragraph, Tolkien's narrator reports:

> The great doors slammed to. Boom. The bars
> of iron fell into place inside. Clang. The gate
> was shut. Sam hurled himself against the bolted
> brazen plates and fell senseless to the ground.
> He was out in the darkness. Frodo was alive but
> taken by the Enemy.

Those wanting to know what happened next had to wait nearly twelve months.

Rayner Unwin would later comment: "For the first and only time in my experience . . . we received letters from individual readers imploring us to put them out of their misery and publish *The Return of the King*. Although I had already ceased to worry about the loss of £1000, it was from these letters from complete strangers that I first realized we had a potential best-seller on our hands."

Though today *The Lord of the Rings* is known only as a worldwide triumph—available in hardback and paperback; in one, three, and seven volumes; and in deluxe, illustrated, boxed, slipcased, and anniversary editions—commercial success came gradually and at times grudgingly, as sales slowly increased over the years, and one by one new translations were made into other languages.

From the start, critical response was mixed, but mixed in a special way. When it came to Tolkien's epic of Middle-earth, there was very little middle ground as critics seemed either to like it very much or very much dislike it—a pattern that has continued to the present.

Using a comparison that has since become well-known, C. S. Lewis wrote that Tolkien's epic was "like lightning from a clear sky." In his review, which appeared in the weekly journal *Time and Tide,* Lewis went on to state: "Here are beauties which pierce like swords or burn like cold iron; here is a book that will break your heart." In a review for *The New York Times*, Auden called *The Lord of the Rings* a masterpiece of its genre.

Other reviewers were of a different opinion. Writing for *The Nation,* American critic Edmund Wilson classified the work as "juvenile trash" and maintained that Tolkien had "little skill at narrative and no instinct for literary form." In a claim that ran counter to the experience of many readers, Wilson asserted that the "poverty of invention" Tolkien displayed seemed "almost pathetic."

Alfred Duggan, the anonymous reviewer for the *Times Literary Supplement,* predicted—entirely incorrectly as it turned out: "This is not a work which many adults will read right through more than once."

In 1961, six years after *The Return of the King* appeared in print, critic Philip Toynbee announced in the London *Observer* that the Rings craze had finally run its course and was passing into "merciful oblivion." In fact, the first huge surge of Hobbit-mania, which took place in the mid and late 1960s, had not yet begun; and in the decades that followed, Tolkien's fiction would enjoy an ever-increasing audience.

"I rarely remember a book about which I have had such violent arguments," Auden wrote in *The New York Times.* "I can only suppose that some people object to heroic quests and imaginary worlds on principle," he wryly concluded. Edmund Fuller offered a different explanation for the unmitigated scorn some critics directed at Tolkien, claiming that it was an "inevitable counter reaction" to the enthusiasm with which his works had been embraced by so many, a natural hazard of their enormous popularity.

Tolkien was well aware of the negative criticism his works generated—once telling Auden that some critics seemed determined to represent him as a "simple-minded adolescent"— but he rarely responded to it. One reason for not responding was because he knew others probably would. An overly harsh attack on Tolkien would typically elicit an even stronger response in his defense. In 1962, after receiving a letter informing him of Philip Toynbee's highly critical review, Tolkien wrote back: "Do not worry too much about Philip Toynbee. Few good reviews can have done me so much commercial benefit. So many people rose up to slay him that the noise was nearly as good as a new book."

One place where Tolkien did respond to his critics, albeit briefly, was in the foreword to the second edition of *The Lord of the Rings*, where he commented: "Some who have read the book, or at any rate have reviewed it, have found it boring, absurd, or contemptible; and I have no cause to complain, since I have similar opinions of their works, or of the kinds of writing that they evidently prefer." Careful readers might note Tolkien's implication that not all of his critics had actually read *The Lord of the Rings* before reviewing it. Tolkien went on to note that the most critical reader of all—the author himself—had found many defects, some major, some minor, but would pass over all of them in silence except for one: "The book is too short," he confessed.

Besides making the book longer, there was one other change Tolkien admitted he would have liked to make. "If I had considered my own pleasure more than the stomachs of a possible audience," he wrote Auden, "there would have been a great deal more Elvish in the book."

On October 15, 1937—just three weeks after the release of *The Hobbit*—Tolkien had confessed to Stanley Unwin that for the past seventeen years he had spent most of his vacations grading exams and doing "things of that sort" due to financial necessity. Unwin's report that a large public would soon be clamoring for more about hobbits had aroused in him a "faint hope" that in the coming years his desire to write and his duty to earn extra money might come together. Not that grading exams was all that profitable, Tolkien went on to note. Even modest book royalties would make a difference. To earn even £100 by grading, he explained, took nearly as much work as writing a full-sized novel.

Unwin wrote back to say that there was good cause for Tolkien's hope. "You are one of those rare people with genius," he explained. "And, unlike some publishers, it is a word I have not used half a dozen times in thirty years of publishing."

Tolkien's hope in 1937 that his writing one day might earn the extra money he needed came true in a far greater way but took far longer than anyone ever imagined. In May 1956, seven months after the release of *The Return of the King*, Tolkien received a check for over £3500, a sum significantly larger than his Oxford salary. And the checks that would arrive in each successive year would be larger and larger.

In July 1972, a little more than a year before his own death, Tolkien was invited to visit the London offices of Allen & Unwin. By this time, he had been retired for many years. In 1968, with more and more unwanted phone calls and unwelcome visits from fans intruding on their privacy, he and Edith had used some of the royalty money to move from Oxford to a more luxurious and more secluded home in Bournemouth— where, for the first time, they enjoyed the luxury of central heating and their own bedrooms. Edith, whose health had become increasingly frail, died in 1971, and afterward Tolkien had moved back to Oxford to a set of rooms offered by his old college. With frequent appearances in the Senior Common Room, dinners at the High Table, and loving care from a college scout and his wife, Tolkien was comfortable.

A car was sent to pick him up at his rooms at 21 Merton Street, and like a member of the royalty, Tolkien was taken to Allen & Unwin's stately new offices in Hemel Hempstead, not to conduct any real business, but for what he later said felt more like an official state visit.

Tolkien, now age eighty, was given a great welcome by

everyone from Accounting to Dispatch and was served, as he noted, a "very good lunch." He was informed that their main business now was connected to sales of *The Hobbit* and *The Lord of the Rings,* which apparently were "rocketing up to hitherto unreached heights." While a single order of one hundred copies was once a big deal, and still was for the other books on Allen & Unwin's list, the firm now was receiving requests for as many as six thousand copies in a single order.

It was a far cry from the first print run of 1,500 copies of *The Hobbit* back in 1937 that Allen & Unwin had hoped to sell, and an even farther cry from the 1,500 copies of *The Fellowship of the Ring* in 1954 that they had expected not to sell.

While Tolkien's publisher had been quite wrong in the prediction that *The Lord of the Rings* might lose money, in a prediction made several years before his death in 1968, Stanley Unwin turned out to be quite correct on another front. Sir Stanley, as he was properly called by then, stated his belief that *The Hobbit* and *The Lord of the Rings* were more likely to outlast his own time and his son's than anything else he had ever published.

—————

In his review of *The Lord of the Rings,* C. S. Lewis addressed a question other critics had raised about Tolkien's use of fantasy as a genre to say something fundamental about the human condition. Why, Lewis asked, if you have a serious comment to make about real life, would you do it in a mythical, heroic, never-never land of your own making? Why not simply write fiction that takes place in the real world? Lewis answered his question this way: "Because, I take it, one of the main things the author wants to say is that the real life of men is of that mythical and heroic quality."

Tolkien's fiction stands in sharp contrast to a century that saw the view of what human beings are and what they are capable of grow smaller and more insignificant. Page after page, chapter after chapter, Tolkien reminds us over and over again that life, our life, is not something small and insignificant but has something mythical and something heroic about it. Each of us has the ability within to do great things, to change the way things are, to make a difference. Or as the narrator in *The Fellowship of the Ring* observes: "There is a seed of courage hidden (often deeply, it is true) in the heart of the fattest and most timid hobbit"—and here we may substitute *human* for *hobbit*—"waiting for some final and desperate danger to make it grow."

And these reminders are crucial.

One reason *The Hobbit* and *The Lord of the Rings* have been so widely popular—both in the previous century and the current one—is because they have been so deeply needed.

123

After a painful night during a visit to see friends in Bournemouth, Tolkien was admitted to a hospital where he was diagnosed with a bleeding gastric ulcer. While the initial reports were optimistic, he developed a chest infection and died two days later on September 2, 1973.

Tolkien was eighty-one.

Four days later he was buried beside Edith at Oxford's Wolvercote Cemetery beneath a simple gravestone that included a reference to Tolkien's cherished story of a love between a mortal man and an elf maiden. It read:

EDITH MARY TOLKIEN

LUTHIEN

1889–1971

JOHN RONALD REUEL TOLKIEN

BEREN

1892–1973

Back in 1951 in the letter to Milton Waldman, Tolkien wrote that once upon a time he had hoped to write a new mythology for England and so began working on his *Book of Lost Tales*, which later became *The Silmarillion*. Tolkien apologized for sounding absurd and admitted his lofty goal of providing a new mythology for his country now seemed laughable.

Edited by his son Christopher and published posthumously in 1977, *The Silmarillion,* despite widespread sales, never gained widespread acceptance and never did become England's mythology. Something far more amazing happened. Tolkien's other two major works—*The Hobbit* and *The Lord of the Rings*—were translated into more than forty different languages and became best-sellers all over the world.

More important, Tolkien's two masterpieces became *beloved* all over the world. They became stories that were read and read again, stories that were passed on from one generation to the next and to the next, reminding us of who we are, why we are here, and what is important in life—and so became a new mythology not just for England, but for everyone.

CURIOUS FACTS OF TOLKIEN'S LIFE AND WRITING

DID YOU KNOW THAT . . . ?

- *The Hobbit* and *The Lord of the Rings* almost did not get published, and both could be described as *books that nearly weren't*.

- It took Tolkien nearly thirteen years to write *The Lord of the Rings,* and he nearly quit several times because he doubted anyone would want to read it.

- The fate of Tolkien's literary future at one point rested with a ten-year-old boy, as the publisher based his decision of whether or not to publish *The Hobbit* on the review given by his young son.

- The three initials in Tolkien's name stand for *John Ronald Reuel*.

- Tolkien was not born in Oxford or in England at all, but a world away in Bloemfontein in the former colony we now know as South Africa.

- Tolkien made it clear that The Shire was based on his memories of his childhood home of Sarehole, England, and his experiences as a young boy growing up there.

- Tolkien's mother died when he was young, and he includes motherless characters throughout his fiction—among them Sam, Boromir and Faramir, Eowyn and Eomer, Arwen, and Frodo.

- Frodo was twelve years old when his parents died in a boating accident, leaving him an orphan at *exactly the age that Tolkien was* when he lost his only surviving parent.

- Tolkien fell in love at the age of eighteen with the young woman who would later become his wife, but he was forbidden to see her for three years until he turned twenty-one.

- The guardian of Tolkien's fiancée was worried Tolkien might not amount to anything and would not be able to support a family.

- During World War I Tolkien was placed in the signal corps, where his Oxford-trained talents as a philologist were put to use learning how to use handheld flags, Morse code, blinking spotlights, and even carrier pigeons to send messages.

- Some of the battle scenes in Tolkien's fiction are based on his own experience at The Battle of the Somme, where he fought in World War I.

- Tolkien's first stories about Middle-Earth were written in the hospital during World War I as he recovered from Trench Fever.

- Tolkien stated in the Preface to *The Lord of the Rings*, "By 1918 all but one of my close friends were dead."

- Before he became an Oxford professor, Tolkien worked on the staff of the *Oxford English Dictionary*, where he wrote the definitions for *waggle, waistcoat, waiter, wallop, walnut, walrus, wampum, wander, wanderer, warm, wasp, warlock, wild, winter,* and *wold.*

- At the age of thirty-three Tolkien became one of the youngest Professors at Oxford.

- Tolkien was awarded not one but *three* successive Professor's chairs—two of them at Oxford.

- Although today a bust of Tolkien is on display at the

college he attended, he nearly was "sent down" or expelled from Oxford because of his poor performance on his "Honor Mods," his first major set of tests.

- Tolkien was grading exams when he came across a blank page and wrote, "In a hole in the ground there lived a hobbit." At the time he had no idea why he wrote it or what a hobbit was. Later it became the opening line of *The Hobbit*.

- Tolkien's original goal in writing stories was to give England a mythology after it lost most of its original legends following the Norman Invasion of 1066.

- *The Lord of the Rings*—the most famous trilogy in the world—was intended by Tolkien to be one big book, not a trilogy.

- The working title for *The Lord of the Rings* was the *New Hobbit*.

- In early drafts of Tolkien's fiction, Gandalf was called Bladorthin, and Frodo was called Bingo.

- When he first wrote the scene where the hobbits meet the cloaked and hooded stranger at the Prancing Pony who would turn out to be Aragorn, Tolkien himself did not know who this strange character was.

- Bilbo's journey over the Misty Mountains is based in part on a hiking trip Tolkien made in the Swiss Alps the summer after he graduated from high school.

- The inspiration for Gandalf came from a painting by the German artist Josef Madlener titled *Der Berggeist*, The Mountain Spirit.

- Tolkien based the two Elvish languages he created on Finnish and Welsh.

- Tolkien's publisher, Allen & Unwin, was sure they were going to lose money on *The Lord of the Rings*.

- At Waterstones, the giant British bookstore, *The Lord of the Rings* was declared the book of the century after it received the most votes at 104 of the store's 105 branches.

- In a poll conducted in the United States, Amazon.com customers voted *The Lord of the Rings* as the best book of the millennium, ahead of such works as *Gone with the Wind,* which came in second, and *To Kill a Mockingbird,* which came in third.

An Unexpected Journey
Fit for Thirteen Dwarves and a Hobbit

FOURTEEN TOLKIEN SITES TO VISIT WITHOUT EVER LEAVING YOUR ARMCHAIR

(Arranged in Chronological Order
of Events in Tolkien's Life)

Tolkien depicts Middle-earth so vividly in his fiction that some readers feel he is describing a real place. Whether you are one of those readers or not, here are fourteen genuinely real places in our own world that have connections to Tolkien.

#1

<u>Where</u>: *Bloemfontein, South Africa*
<u>What</u>: *Tolkien's Birthplace and the Grave
        of Arthur Tolkien*

Following their marriage in 1891, Arthur and Mabel Tolkien moved into the rooms above the bank on Maitland Street where Arthur worked. Mabel gave birth to their first son—John Ronald Reuel—in this home on January 3, 1892. The original Bank House building is now gone, having been wiped out by a flood and replaced by a new structure in 1933. While Mabel and the two boys were on a visit to England, Arthur contracted rheumatic fever and died on February 15, 1896. Five days afterward, his body was laid to rest in Bloemfontein's Anglican graveyard. In the early 1990s members of the South African Tolkien Society located Arthur's grave and, along with the Tolkien family, had a new gravestone placed on it.

#2

Where: Sarehole, England
What: Tolkien's Boyhood Home

In the summer of 1896, Mabel Tolkien and her two young sons moved to what is now Number 264 Wake Green in Sarehole, a small hamlet consisting of a handful of farms and houses nestled alongside the River Cole. The Shire was based on Tolkien's memories of Sarehole and his experiences during the four years his family lived there. In an interview he explained: "I took the idea of the hobbits from the village people and children. I was brought up in considerable poverty, but I was happy running about in that country." Visitors today can still see Sarehole Mill much as it was when Tolkien lived there. Constructed around 1750, it is one of only two surviving working watermills in the Birmingham area.

#3

Where: Birmingham, England
What: King Edward's School

In September 1900 at the age of eight and a half Tokien was admitted to begin classes at the prestigious King Edward's School in Birmingham. Although two years later he was awarded a Foundation Scholarship, initially his tuition of £12 per year was paid for by one of his uncles. It was here that—when he was not on the soccer field—Tolkien developed his linguistic skills and his love for ancient myths. It was also here that, along with three school friends, he created the T.C.B.S.—the Tea Club, Barrovian Society—a literary club where the great epics as well as the club members' own compositions were read aloud and discussed.

#4

Where: *Exeter College, Oxford*
What: *Tolkien's College as an Undergraduate*

In October 1911 Tolkien enrolled as a freshman at Exeter College on a scholarship to read Classics. He was given college lodgings on the corner of Turl Street and Broad Street in a building which no longer exists. In 1913, after a poor performance on one of his first major tests, Tolkien was advised to change from Classics to English Language and Literature, and in 1915 he graduated with first class honors. Visitors today will find a bust of Tolkien on prominent display near the entrance to the college's beautiful Victorian chapel. Cast in bronze from the plaster version made by Faith Tolkien, the author's daughter-in-law, it pays tribute to Exeter's most famous son.

#5

Where: *Old Ashmolean Building, Broad Street, Oxford*
What: *The Former Home of the* Oxford English Dictionary

After graduating from Exeter, Tolkien served as an officer in WWI, where he was wounded in the Battle of the Somme. After his recovery, Tolkien was invited to work on the *Oxford English Dictionary*, a project that at the time was housed in the

Old Ashmolean Building. In January 1919, Tolkien began as an assistant lexicographer and was assigned words beginning with W. Long after Tolkien's stint at the dictionary was over, two new words from his fiction were deemed to have achieved currency in English, and because of this, hobbit and orc were added to the *OED*.

#6

Where: *Leeds University, England*
What: *The First University Where Tolkien Taught*

In 1920 Tolkien was offered a post at Leeds University, about 160 miles north of Oxford, where he taught for the next five years. Beginning first at the rank of Reader, Tolkien was appointed to a new Professorship in English Language in 1924. During his time at Leeds, Tolkien collaborated with E. V. Gordon on a new edition of the Middle English poem *Sir Gawain and the Green Knight*, which would go on to become the most widely used text of the poem studied in Britain and the U.S. Together Tolkien and Gordon also helped to found the Leeds Viking Club, an organization dedicated to singing and reading Old Icelandic sagas, as well as to a good deal of beer drinking and merriment.

#7

Where: Pembroke College, Oxford
What: The First College in Oxford Where Tolkien
Was a Professor

In the summer of 1925, a position at Oxford became open. Knowing that his candidacy was a long shot, Tolkien carefully crafted a letter dated June 27 to the Electors of the Rawlinson and Bosworth Professorship of Anglo-Saxon, which began: "Gentlemen, I desire to offer myself as a candidate." To his great surprise, the thirty-three-year-old Tolkien beat out the other contenders and was offered the prestigious position, which was housed at Pembroke College. Tolkien moved his family from Leeds back to Oxford and remained at this position for the next twenty years, leaving it in 1945 to become a Professor at Merton College.

#8

Where: 20 Northmoor Road, Oxford
What: Tolkien's Home Where The Hobbit
and The Lord of the Rings Were Written

In an interview, Tolkien recalled the events of a warm summers' day in 1930; "I can still see the corner of my house in 20 Northmoor Road where it happened. I had an enormous pile of exam papers there. Marking school examinations in the summertime is very laborious and unfortunately also boring. And I remember picking up a paper and actually finding—I nearly gave an extra mark for it; an extra five marks actually—there was one page of this particular paper that was left blank. Glorious! Nothing to read. So I scribbled on it, I can't think why: In a hole in the ground there lived a hobbit." This became the opening line for *The Hobbit*. Tolkien and his family lived at number 20 from 1930 to 1947, and it was here that both *The Hobbit* and *The Lord of the Rings* were written.

#9

<u>Where</u>: *Merton College, Oxford*
<u>What</u>: *The Second College in Oxford Where Tolkien Was a Professor*

For the vast majority of his life, Tolkien supported himself and his family by teaching—not by writing. From 1945 to 1959, he was Professor of English Language and Literature at Merton College, one of the oldest colleges in the world, having been founded in the thirteenth century. Merton possesses a magnificent dining hall that was built in 1277. Over the centuries it has hosted many historic figures, among them Queen Elizabeth I. When in college, Tolkien ate his meals at the High

Table. Dating from 1373, Merton also has the oldest continuously functioning academic library in the world, and it was here that Tolkien did a great deal of his reading and research.

#10

Where: **The Eagle and Child Pub,**
St. Giles Street, Oxford
What: **The Meeting Place of the Inklings**

A gathering of friends of Tolkien and C. S. Lewis, the Oxford Inklings met regularly throughout the 1930s and 1940s for general conversation and for readings and criticism of their own works—among them *The Hobbit* and *The Lord of the Rings.* On Thursday evenings the Inklings met in Lewis's rooms in Magdalen College. On Tuesday mornings they met in various Oxford pubs, but most often at The Eagle and Child, also known as The Bird and Baby. "Properly speaking," wrote Warren Lewis, the brother of the famous author and one of their number, the Inklings "was neither a club nor a literary society, though it partook of the nature of both. There were no rules, officers, agendas, or formal elections." Founded in 1650, The Eagle and Child continues to serve a wide variety of drinks on tap as well as traditional pub food.

#11

Where: *Magdalen College, Oxford*
What: *Addison's Walk*

Before the Inklings were formed, Tolkien met with just Lewis to read aloud his stories from *The Book of Lost Tales.* "He was for long my only audience," Tolkien explained. "Only from him did I ever get the idea that my 'stuff' could be more than a private hobby." It is certain that without Lewis's encouragement, there would have been no Lord of the Rings, for when Tolkien got discouraged and stopped altogether, Lewis was always there insisting on more. Likewise, it was through Tolkien's assistance that Lewis, a serious atheist at the time, came to a belief in Christ—in part through a late-night stroll and discussion that took place on Addison's Walk on September 19, 1931.

#12

Where: *Rose Lane, Oxford*
What: *The University of Oxford Botanic Garden*

Famous for his love of trees and growing things, Tolkien spent a good deal of time in the Oxford Botanic Garden—the oldest botanic garden in Great Britain and one of the oldest scientific gardens in the world. Founded nearly four hundred years ago in 1621, it contains over five thousand different plant species on less than five acres of land, making it one of the most biodiverse places on Earth. The last photograph of Tolkien, taken here in 1972 just eleven months before his death, shows him leaning against his favorite tree—the twisty, deformed Black Pine. Grown from a seed planted in the 1790s, it was this enormous pine that served as the inspiration for the Ents in *The Lord of the Rings*. Still growing there today, the tree looks as if it is about to stand up and walk.

#13

Where: 21 Merton Street, Oxford
What: Tolkien's Last Residence

In 1968, with an increasing number of unwanted phone calls and visits from fans intruding on their privacy, Tolkien and his wife, Edith, used some of the royalty money that had started to come in to move from Oxford to a more luxurious and more secluded home in Bournemouth—where for the first time they enjoyed the luxury of central heating and their own bedrooms. Edith, whose health had become increasingly frail, died in 1971. Afterward Tolkien moved back to Oxford to a set of rooms offered by his old college at 21 Merton Street. With frequent appearances in the Merton Senior Common Room, dinners at the High Table, and loving care from a college scout and his wife, Tolkien was comfortable here for the remaining months of his life.

#14

Where: **Wolvercote Cemetery, Oxford**
What: **Tolkien's Gravesite**

Edith Tolkien died on November 29, 1971, at the age of eighty-two. When Tolkien died twenty-one months later on September 2, 1973, at the age of eighty-one, he was buried in the same grave. The Tolkiens' final resting place is Wolvercote Cemetery, located on the outskirts of Oxford. Their simple gravestone includes the inscription Luthien under Edith's name and Beren below his own—two characters from *The Silmarillion*, which was edited by Tolkien's son Christopher Tolkien and published in 1977. In Tolkien's mythology of Middle-earth, the mortal man Beren fell in love with the beautiful Elf-maiden Luthien after seeing her dancing in a moonlit glade.

RESOURCES

Carpenter, Humphrey. *J. R. R. Tolkien: A Biography*. New York: Houghton Mifflin, 2000.

Garth, John. *Tolkien and the Great War: The Threshold of Middle-earth*. New York: Houghton Mifflin, 2003.

Lewis, C. S. *Letters of C. S. Lewis*. New York: Harcourt Brace, 1993.

Pearce, Joseph. *Tolkien: Man and Myth*. London: HarperCollins, 1999.

Scull, Christina and Wayne G. Hammond. *The J. R. R. Tolkien Companion and Guide: Chronology*. New York: Houghton Mifflin, 2006.

Tolkien, J. R. R. *The Fellowship of the Ring*. New York: Houghton Mifflin, 1994.

———. "Foreword to the First Edition." *The Fellowship of the Ring*. London: Allen & Unwin, 1954. 7–8.

———. "Foreword to the Second Edition." *The Fellowship of the Ring*. New York: Houghton Mifflin, 1994. xiii–xvi.

———. *The Hobbit*. New York: Houghton Mifflin, 1994.

RESOURCES

——. *The Letters of J. R. R. Tolkien.* Ed. Humphrey Carpenter. New York: Houghton Mifflin, 2000.

——. "On Fairy-Stories." *The Monsters and the Critics and Other Essays.* New York: HarperCollins, 2006. 109–61.

——. *The Return of the King.* New York: Houghton Mifflin, 1994.

——. *The Silmarillion.* Ed. Christopher Tolkien. New York: Houghton Mifflin, 1981.

——. *The Two Towers.* New York: Houghton Mifflin, 1994.

Unwin, Rayner. *George Allen & Unwin A Remembrancer.* Ludlow, England: Merlin Unwin Books, 1999.

A Book for the Hobbit in Each of Us

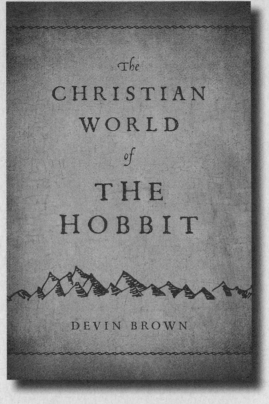

Hardcover | 9781630888190 | $24.99
Paperback | 9781426749490 | $14.99
E-Book | 9781426759864 | $14.99

Discover a side of Tolkien that is rarely explored but vitally important to his writings—his faith. This approachable, witty, and highly entertaining book offers up fresh perspectives to fans of *The Hobbit*, both the book and the film adaptation.

Available wherever books are sold

Abingdon Press

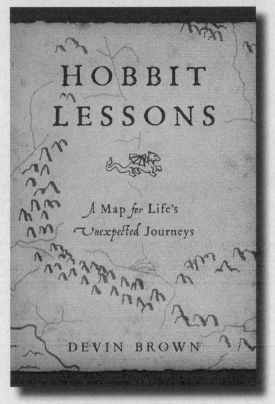

Take a Look Inside the Wardrobe

More satisfying than Turkish Delight, with Lion-Sized Relevance, *Bringing Narnia Home* is a wise, winsome and whimsical exploration of the lessons found on the other side of the wardrobe.

Hardcover | 9781501800030 | $24.99
Paperback | 9781416791628 | $12.99
E-Book | 9781426791628 | $12.99

Whether you're a longtime fan of The Chronicles of Narnia or are just discovering them for the first time, you will be amazed and inspired as you undertake your very own chapter-by-chapter tour through *The Lion, the Witch, and the Wardrobe*.

Paperback | 9781426787133 | $14.99
E-Book | 9781426785559 | $14.99

If you have only traveled to Narnia through the wardrobe, there is so much more to explore. Join Peter, Susan, Edmund, and Lucy on a guided tour of their second trip to the magical land.

Paperback | 9781426787201 | $14.99
E-Book | 9781426785610 | $14.99

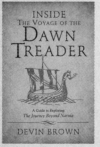

This tale about Narnia takes readers on a high-seas adventure to places beyond the imagination filled with new characters and new conflicts. Take a look behind the scenes of *The Voyage of the Dawn Treader*.

Paperback | 9781426787218 | $14.99
E-Book | 9781426785603 | $14.99

Available wherever books are sold

◖d┃Abingdon Press™